LIFE DRAWING
Anatomy and live models

THOMAS WIENC

A & C Black • London

Published in Great Britain 2011
A&C Black Publishers
36 Soho Square
London W1D 3QY
www.acblack.com

ISBN: 978-1-4081-3452-8

First published in France in 2010
Copyright © Dessain and Tolra/Larousse 2010

A CIP catalogue record for this book is available from the British Library

Thomas Wienc has asserted his rights under the Copyright, Design and Patents Act,
1988, to be identified as the author of this work.

Editorial director: Colette Hanicotte
Editor: Corinne de Montalembert
Editorial assistant: Natalia Dobiecka
Page design: Florence Le Maux
Production: Anne Raynaud
English text layout: Susan McIntyre
Translation: Alexa Stace
Assistant editor, English edition: Ellen Parnavelas
Cover design: James Watson

This book is produced using paper that is made from wood grown in managed,
sustainable forests. It is natural, renewable and recyclable. The logging
and manufacturing processes conform to the environmental regulations
of the country of origin.

Printed and bound in China

Introduction

This manual of life drawing for students is mainly intended for beginners. In it, I try to emphasise the graphic elements that seem to me to be the most important when depicting the human body. Thus it will be a question of muscles and bones of course, but also of tendons, fat and folds of skin, for all of these have a role to play in this depiction.

By analysing chosen drawings, each chapter illustrates a principle to be memorised, or effects to look out for. Lessons are based on observable elements, rather than on information that requires exhaustive anatomical knowledge.

In fact, in this work I have deliberately highlighted some anatomical facts, but left aside others that could have been included. Given the limited number of pages to treat this vast subject, there is not space enough to include examples of how not to do things. I have mostly avoided descriptive drawings of the skeleton. It seemed to me more useful to concentrate on the external shapes, accepting the risk of being a little simplistic. This is why the bone structure often appears to include very simplified pathways. I have almost always kept the correct nomenclature for muscles and bones, and, above all, have tried to represent their directions accurately.

My suggested methods derive from personal experience, but are not intended to be obligatory. I regularly see excellent drawings done in many different ways, sometimes based only on instinct and feeling, without any particular method or knowledge. Nevertheless, from personal experience I would urge that an organised approach, more thoughtful and less impulsive, offers a more consistent result.

Most of the drawings presented here have been done in situ, during courses with students or in similar situations, then reworked to illustrate a point. Their style is not of interest in itself: they serve to put forward the necessary techniques for illustrating the body. In other words, there is no artistic intention in this approach; it is a box of tools rather than a catalogue of art drawings. Basically, these are sketches executed in one go, in 25 minutes, in A4 format. The drawings have been done with coloured pencils, but also with felt-tip pens, and none of them have been retouched. An apprenticeship in the different pictorial techniques, for example, skills such as highlighting, is not proposed in this work. Nevertheless, the information presented here could be used for a personal pictorial approach.

Finally, I must explain the very small percentage of drawings showing different physiognomies. I say this, knowing that African or Asian models for example are hardly shown in my work, and this was not my wish. As I have already said, the drawings shown here were mostly done during courses, and unfortunately this restricted the models available.

Caricature of Thomas Wienc
by Matthieu Pitschon.

3

Contents

Equipment

You do not need much equipment to start life drawing. If you are a beginner, I would advise you to begin with the dry techniques – for example, crayons, pastels, chalks – as it is these that I have used in this book.

Choose good quality coloured pencils.

Crayons, pastels, charcoal and chalk will all need to be sprayed with an aerosol fixative when your work is finished.

I like stabilo highlighter pens for their modern, luminous appearance.

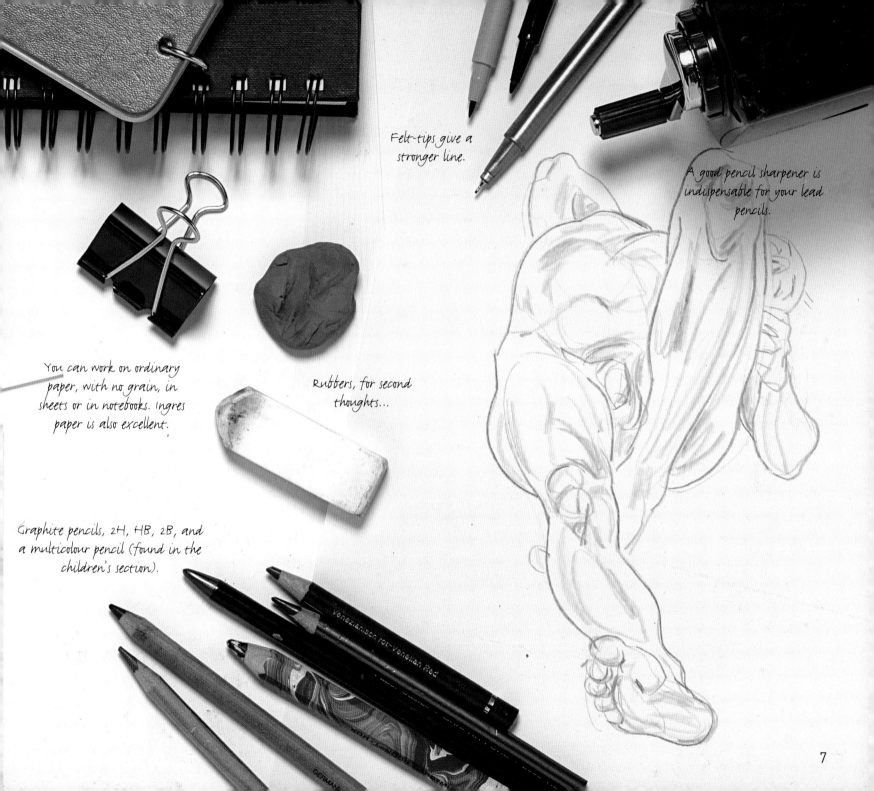

Felt-tips give a stronger line.

A good pencil sharpener is indispensable for your lead pencils.

You can work on ordinary paper, with no grain, in sheets or in notebooks. Ingres paper is also excellent.

Rubbers, for second thoughts...

Graphite pencils, 2H, HB, 2B, and a multicolour pencil (found in the children's section).

7

Position yourself in relation to the subject

Looking straight ahead, find a horizontal line at eye level to use as a reference point. Observe where this line crosses the figure in front of you.

In the portion of the figure that is above your eye-line, the parts closest to you will appear highest in your drawing, and those furthest away must be placed lowest. For the portion of the figure below the line, the nearest elements will be positioned the lowest in your drawing. Note, however, that as the torso is flexible, the axis of the shoulders can be in a contrary direction to this rule.

In this view, the line of the horizon is above the model's head. Thus all the vanishing lines are slanted in the same direction.

Line of the horizon.

A little trap: here the right thigh of the model is contracted and so the kneecap is higher. In this case the height of the knees does not make a reliable reference point for the perspective.

High kneecap; muscular mass contracted.

Low kneecap; muscular mass relaxed.

Above all, pay attention to the different height of the feet in standing poses.

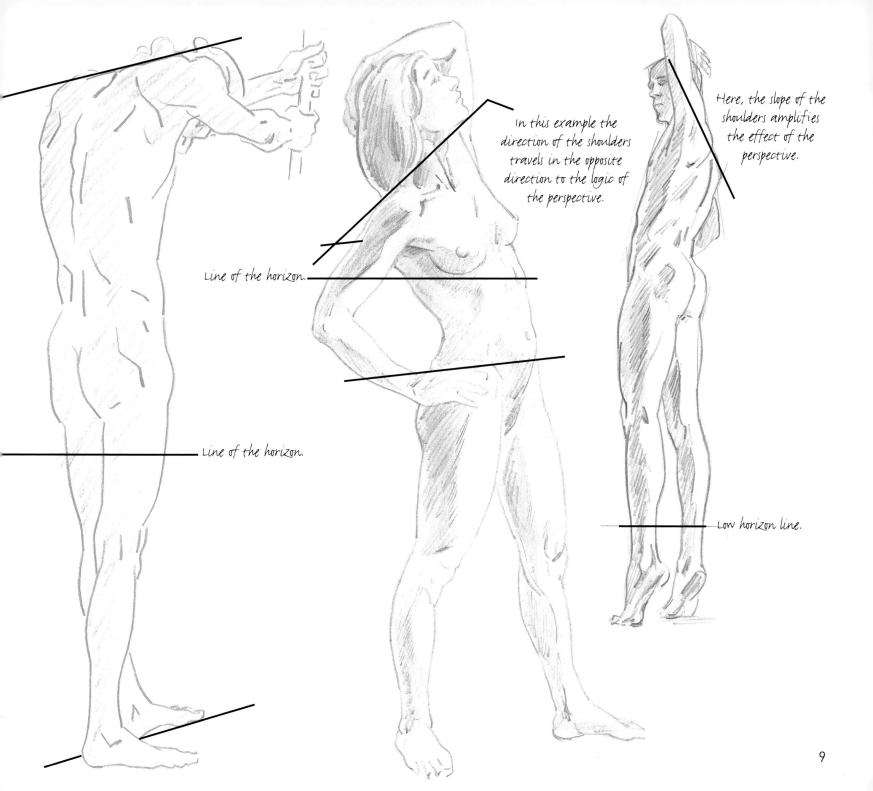

In this example the direction of the shoulders travels in the opposite direction to the logic of the perspective.

Here, the slope of the shoulders amplifies the effect of the perspective.

Line of the horizon.

Line of the horizon.

Low horizon line.

9

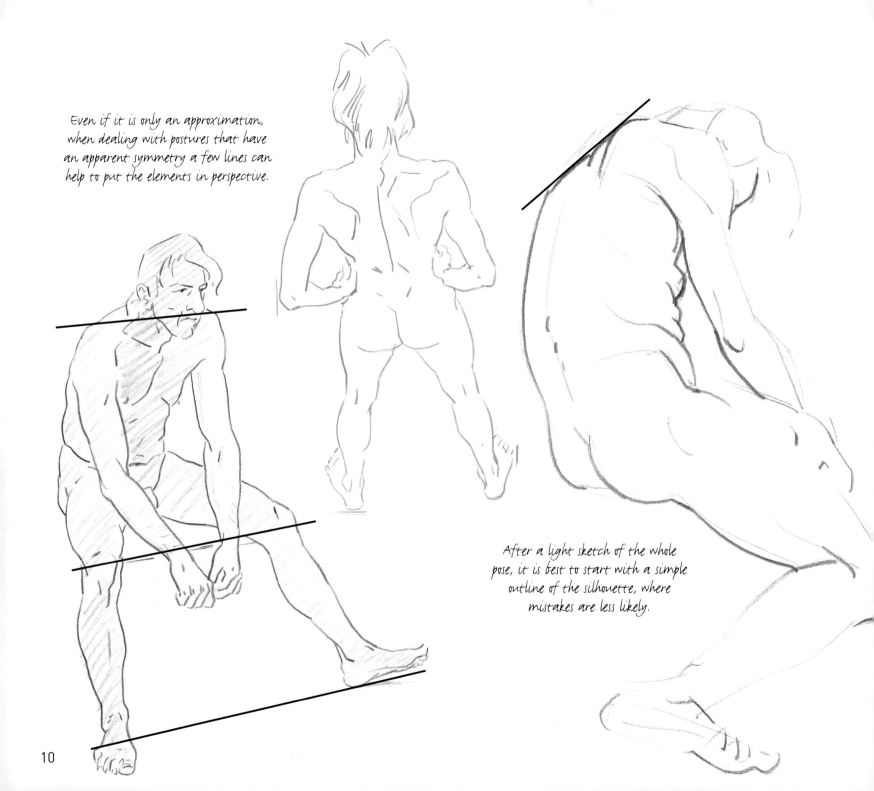

Even if it is only an approximation,
when dealing with postures that have
an apparent symmetry a few lines can
help to put the elements in perspective.

After a light sketch of the whole
pose, it is best to start with a simple
outline of the silhouette, where
mistakes are less likely.

In this kind of pose, it is best to favour other reference points, and it may help to put in a simple geometric shape, by looking for connections.

When the model stretches out, it is most often entirely under the line of the horizon. Thus, follow the rules of perspective for all points in contact with the ground plan: the nearest parts will be placed lowest in the drawing; those stretched furthest away, placed the highest.

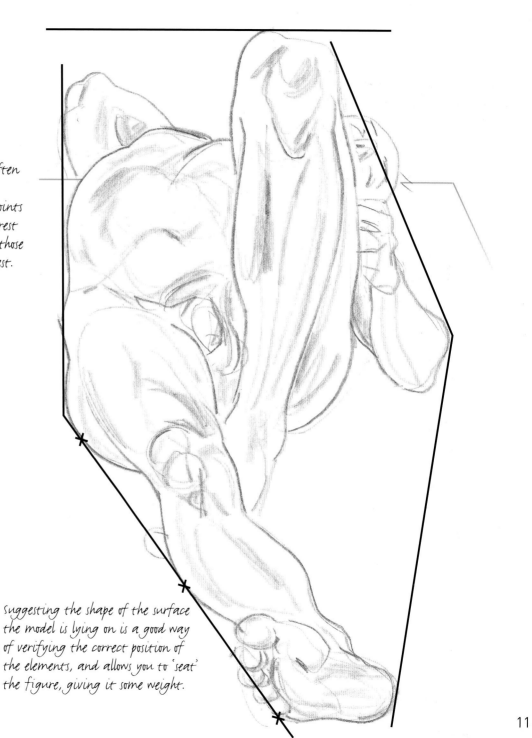

suggesting the shape of the surface the model is lying on is a good way of verifying the correct position of the elements, and allows you to 'seat' the figure, giving it some weight.

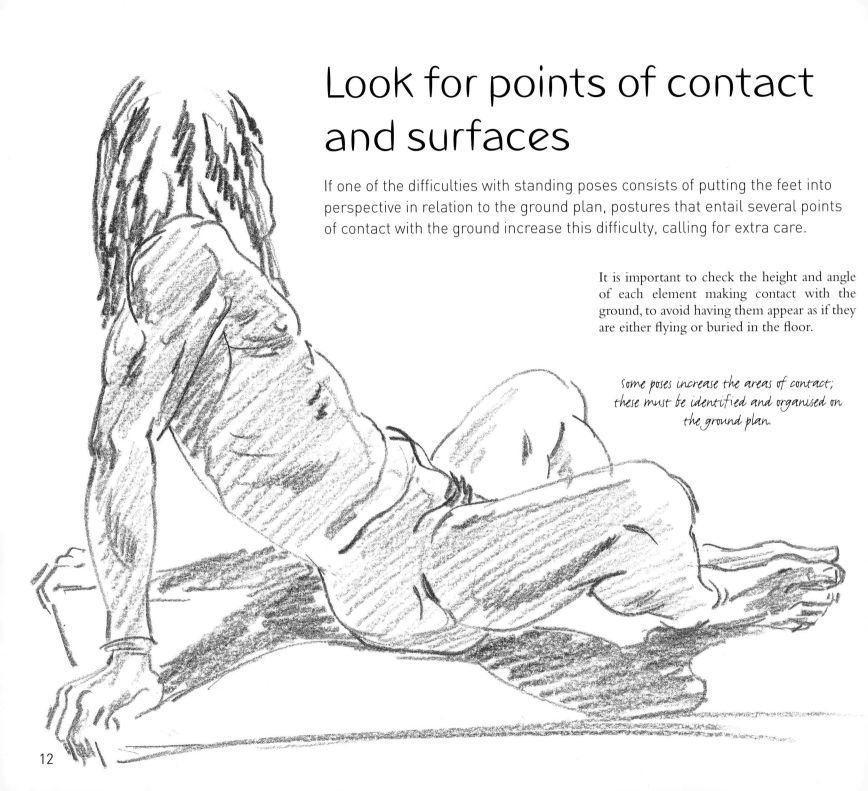

Look for points of contact and surfaces

If one of the difficulties with standing poses consists of putting the feet into perspective in relation to the ground plan, postures that entail several points of contact with the ground increase this difficulty, calling for extra care.

It is important to check the height and angle of each element making contact with the ground, to avoid having them appear as if they are either flying or buried in the floor.

Some poses increase the areas of contact; these must be identified and organised on the ground plan.

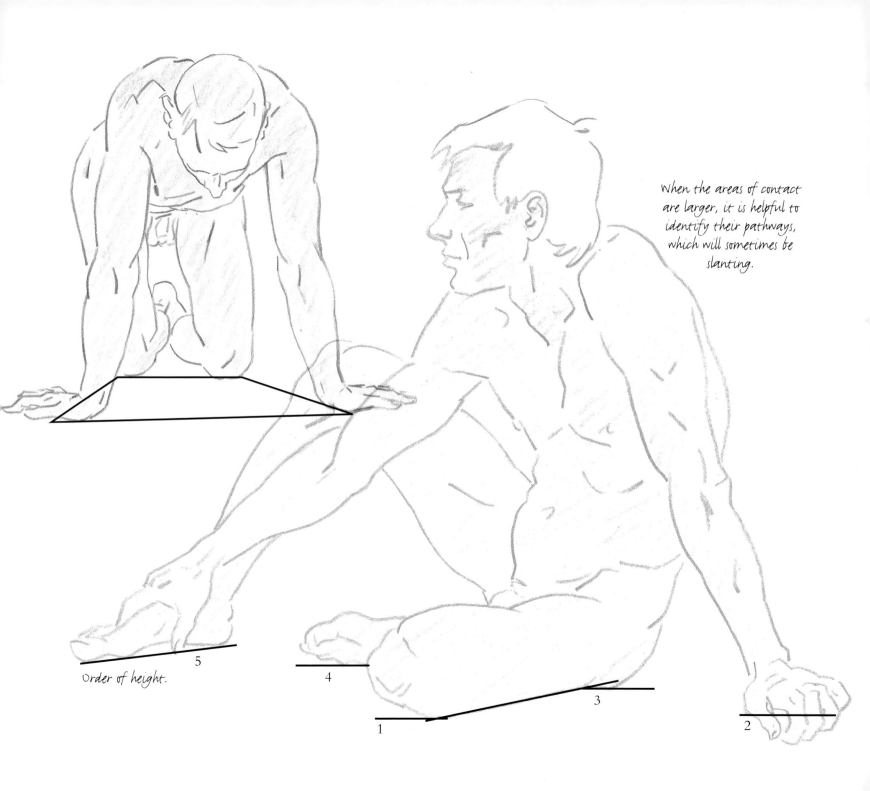

When the areas of contact are larger, it is helpful to identify their pathways, which will sometimes be slanting.

Order of height.

5

4

1

3

2

1

2

3

4

The correct arrangement of these reference points is essential for the figure to appear balanced. Always apply the rules of perspective.

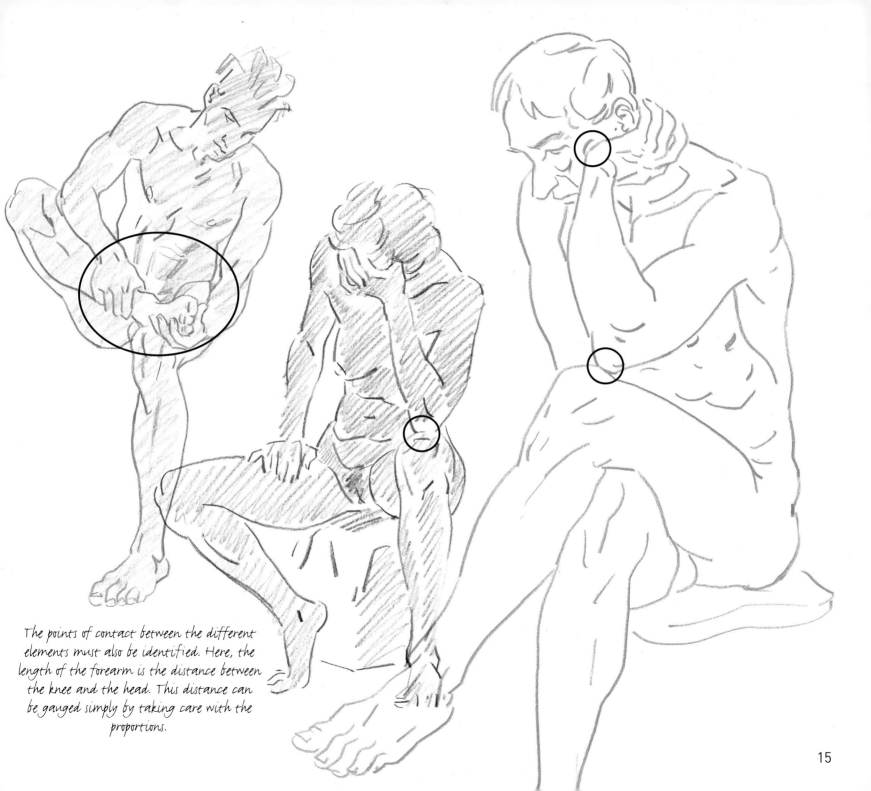

The points of contact between the different elements must also be identified. Here, the length of the forearm is the distance between the knee and the head. This distance can be gauged simply by taking care with the proportions.

15

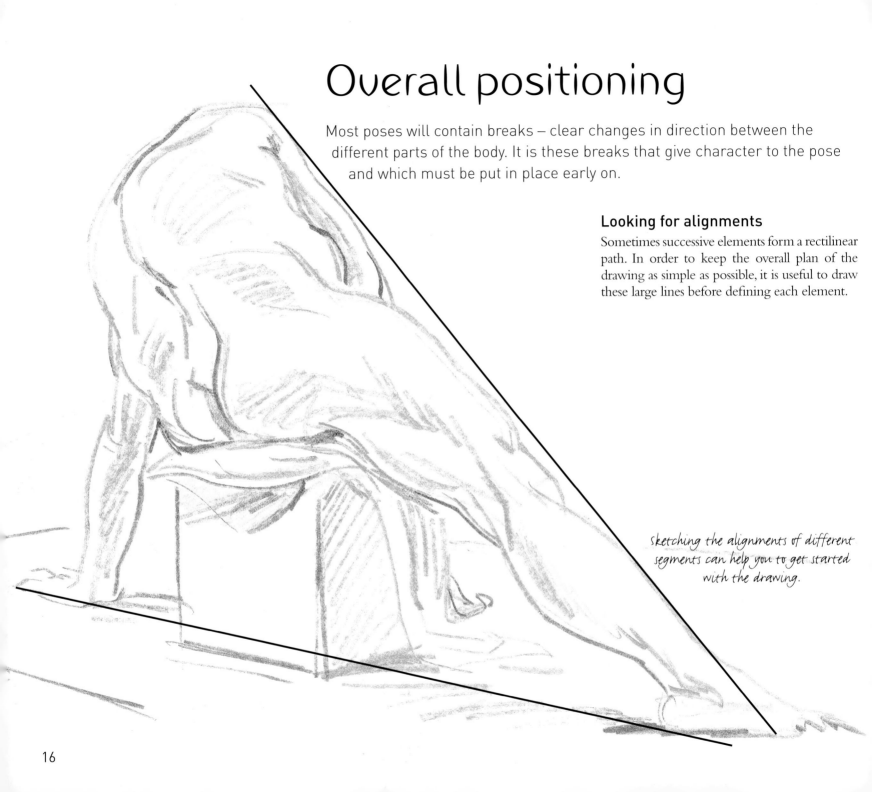

Overall positioning

Most poses will contain breaks – clear changes in direction between the different parts of the body. It is these breaks that give character to the pose and which must be put in place early on.

Looking for alignments

Sometimes successive elements form a rectilinear path. In order to keep the overall plan of the drawing as simple as possible, it is useful to draw these large lines before defining each element.

sketching the alignments of different segments can help you to get started with the drawing.

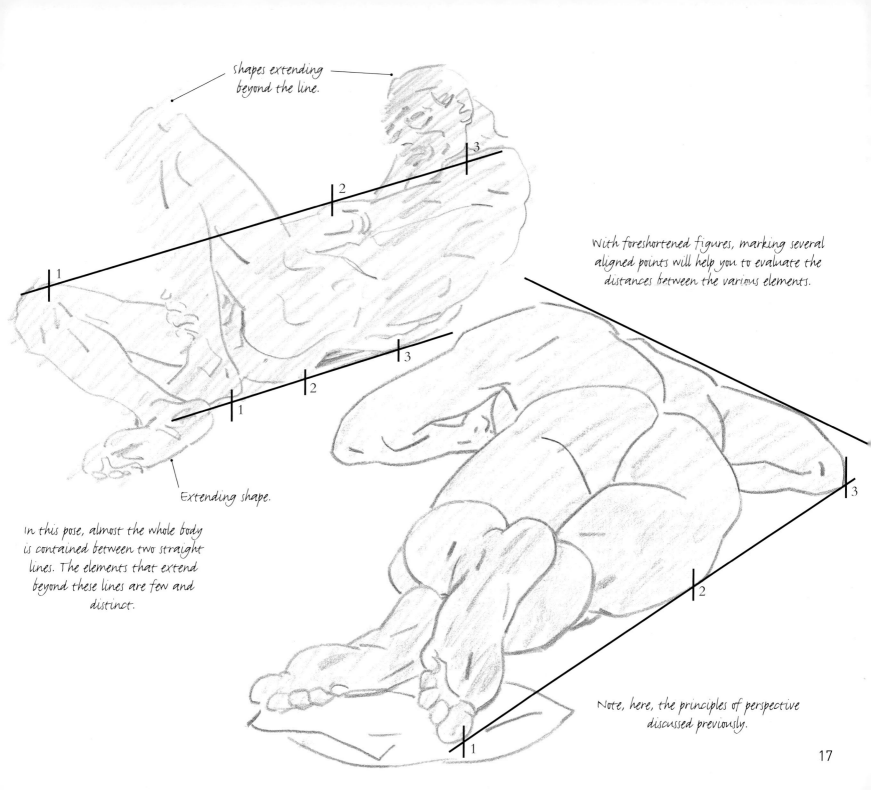

shapes extending
beyond the line.

With foreshortened figures, marking several
aligned points will help you to evaluate the
distances between the various elements.

Extending shape.

In this pose, almost the whole body
is contained between two straight
lines. The elements that extend
beyond these lines are few and
distinct.

Note, here, the principles of perspective
discussed previously.

17

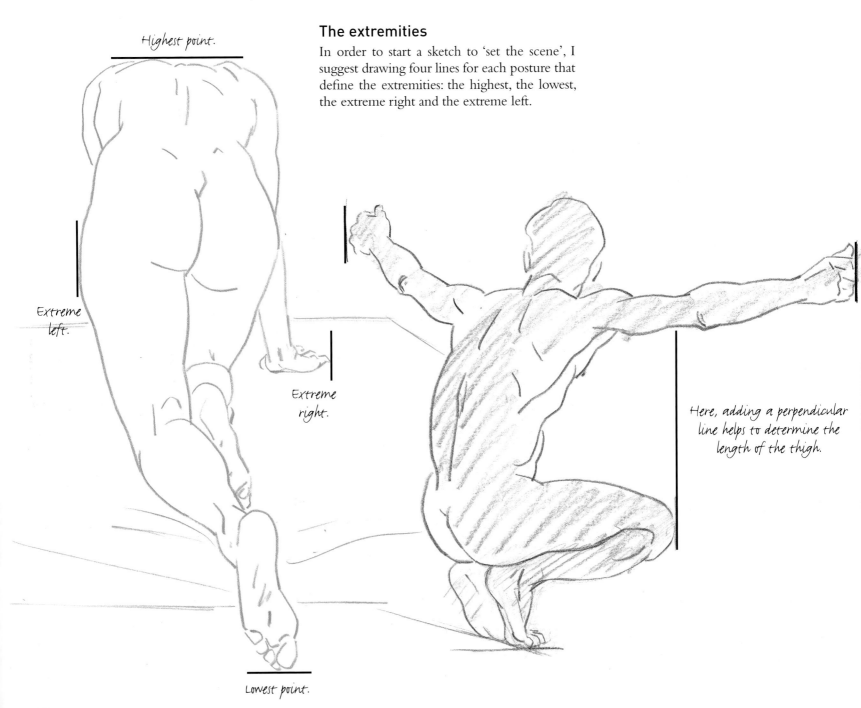

Highest point.

The extremities

In order to start a sketch to 'set the scene', I suggest drawing four lines for each posture that define the extremities: the highest, the lowest, the extreme right and the extreme left.

Extreme left.

Extreme right.

Here, adding a perpendicular line helps to determine the length of the thigh.

Lowest point.

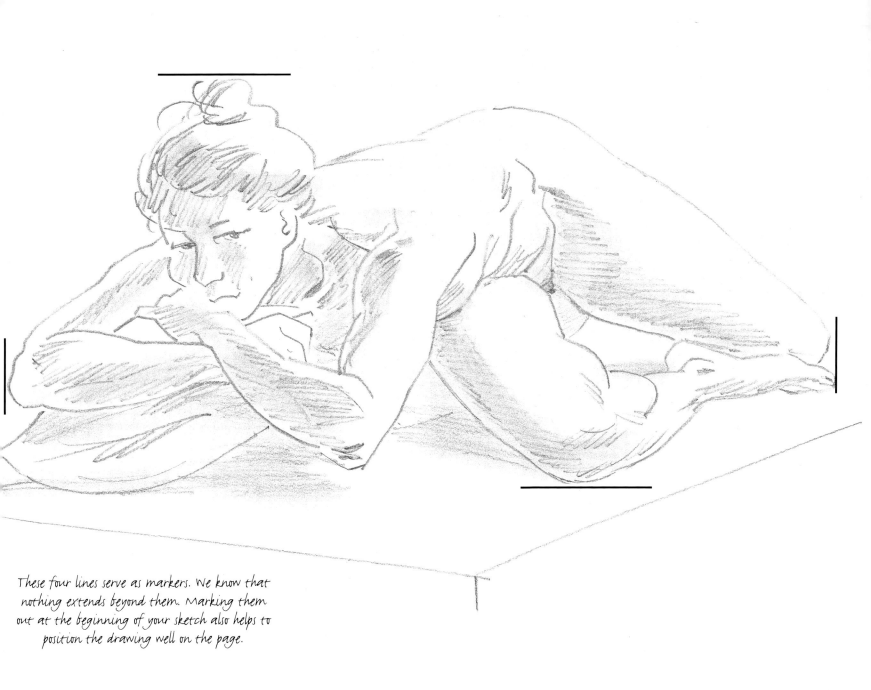

These four lines serve as markers. We know that
nothing extends beyond them. Marking them
out at the beginning of your sketch also helps to
position the drawing well on the page.

19

Angles

To contrast with the straight lines, I find it interesting to place the most obvious angular shapes, often the elbows or knees, after the initial outline has been made, to give a dynamic feel to the sketch.

The lines drawn over this sketch show the breaks between the segments. The more curved forms that emerge from these pathways can be added after the main outline is complete.

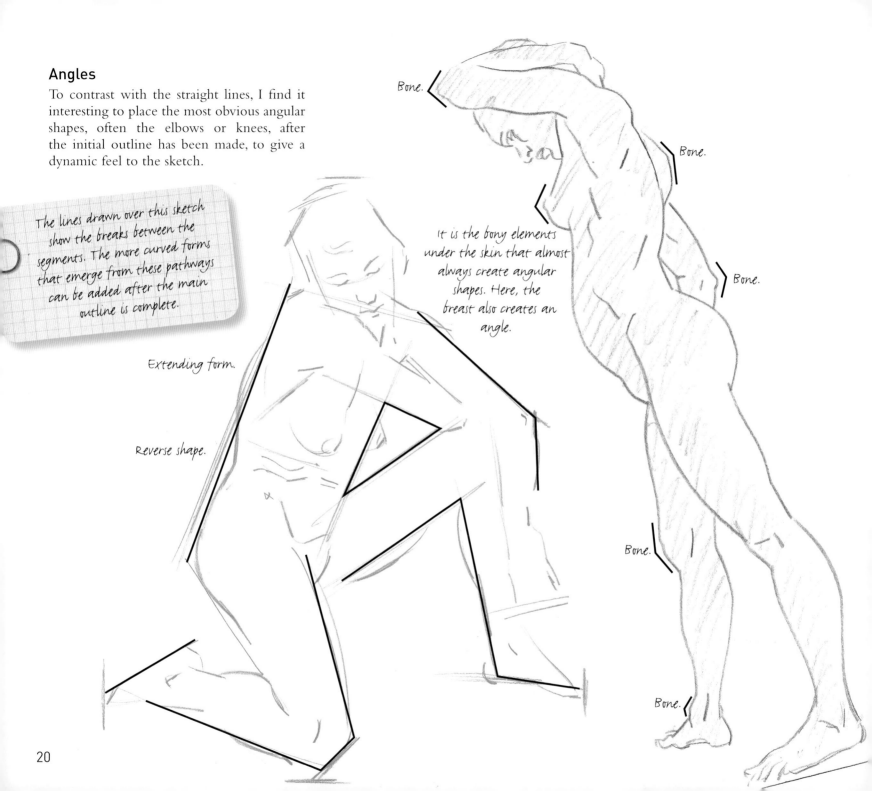

Bone.

Bone.

Bone.

It is the bony elements under the skin that almost always create angular shapes. Here, the breast also creates an angle.

Bone.

Extending form.

Reverse shape.

Bone.

Bone.

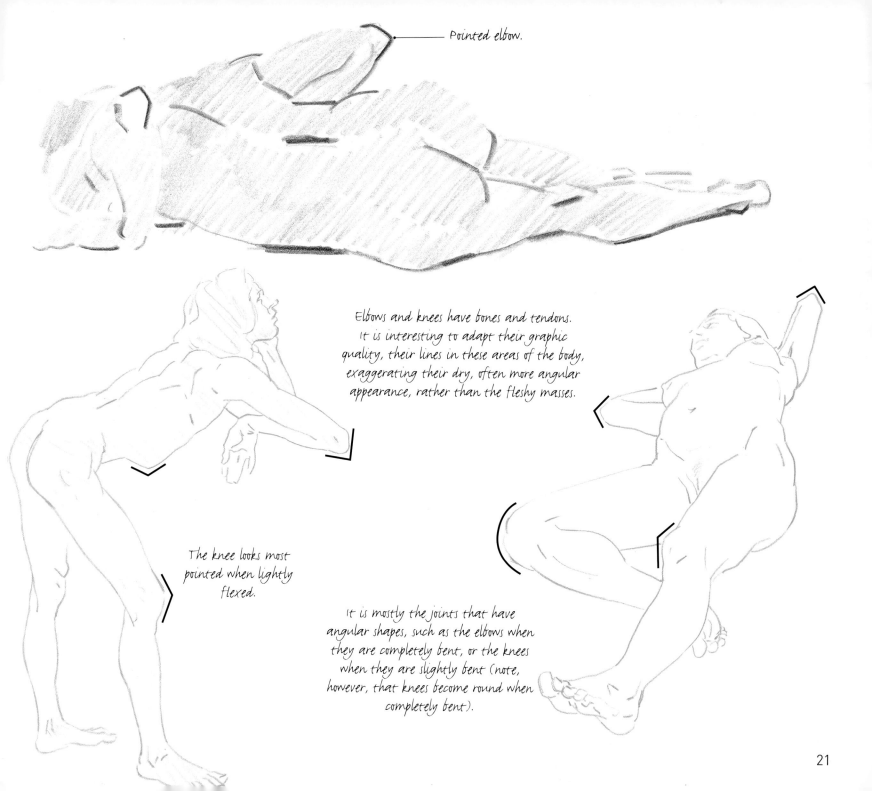

Pointed elbow.

Elbows and knees have bones and tendons. It is interesting to adapt their graphic quality, their lines in these areas of the body, exaggerating their dry, often more angular appearance, rather than the fleshy masses.

The knee looks most pointed when lightly flexed.

It is mostly the joints that have angular shapes, such as the elbows when they are completely bent, or the knees when they are slightly bent (note, however, that knees become round when completely bent).

Adding details, but not too early

It is best to avoid starting the drawing with a detail, such as the face or another body part that involves a real investment in time. It is better to draw the whole outline which you can then add to bit by bit. Before adding detail, check that the connection between all of the elements is correct. The ideal is to be able to make changes right up to the last moment. This outline can stay very light, hardly visible, so that you can change the position of elements without spoiling the drawing.

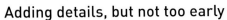

I sketch out a silhouette in grey around which I add some profiles and to which I add the details that seem most important.

Pectoral.

Latissimus dorsi.

For a more atmospheric drawing, try making strokes in medium grey, to indicate shaded parts, leave the white of the paper to indicate highlights, then put in darker strokes to create a third value. It is not necessary to finish the figure completely when using this technique.

The shaded area can be outlined with dark edging, which will reinforce, by contrast, the effect of the light. When drawing with highlights, avoid too regular an outline for the best results.

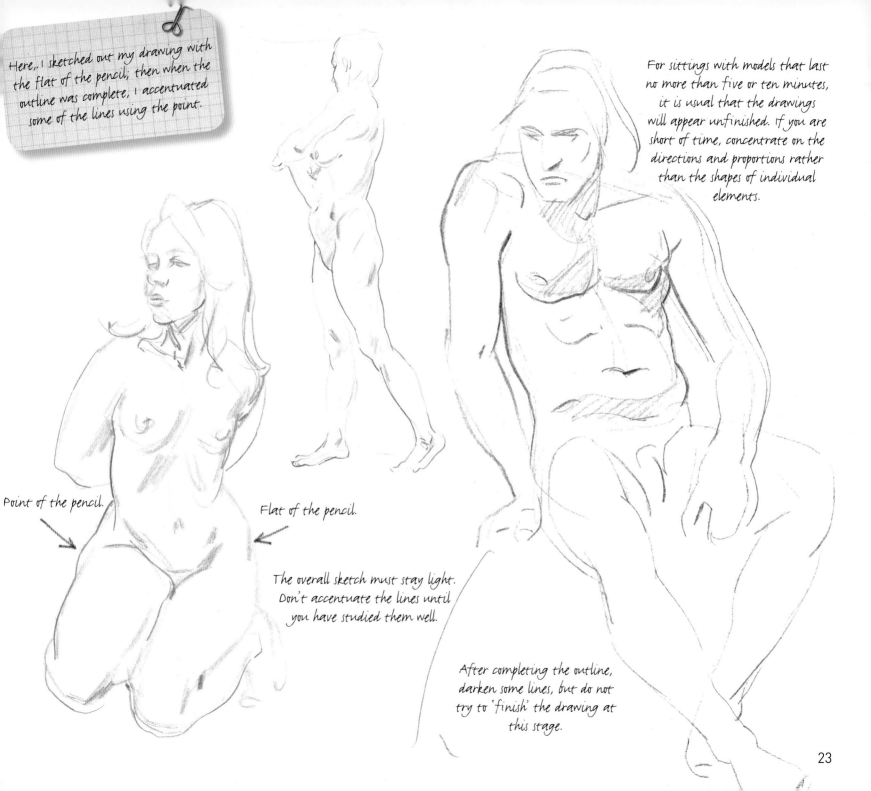

Here, I sketched out my drawing with the flat of the pencil; then when the outline was complete, I accentuated some of the lines using the point.

For sittings with models that last no more than five or ten minutes, it is usual that the drawings will appear unfinished. If you are short of time, concentrate on the directions and proportions rather than the shapes of individual elements.

Point of the pencil.

Flat of the pencil.

The overall sketch must stay light. Don't accentuate the lines until you have studied them well.

After completing the outline, darken some lines, but do not try to 'finish' the drawing at this stage.

23

Curves and straight lines

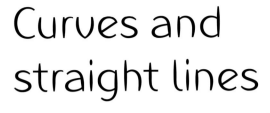

The human body is a combination of curved shapes and straight tendons. Hollows such as the armpit are created by the surrounding volumes and therefore never appear in silhouette. The illusion of a hollow can be created by two successive curves forming a very open angle, or by a tendon following the shape of a muscle.

The principle

Imagine that there are no hollows – in other words, don't indicate hollows in the outlines of your drawing.

If you look closely, you will see that the silhouette is almost never hollowed out.

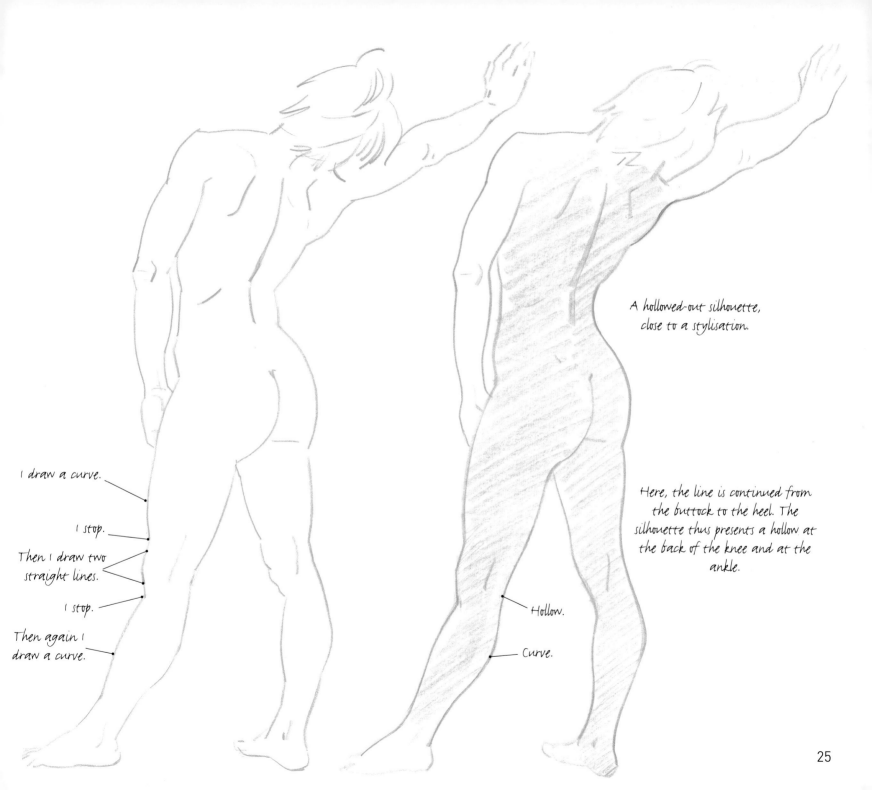

I draw a curve.

I stop.

Then I draw two
straight lines.

I stop.

Then again I
draw a curve.

A hollowed-out silhouette,
close to a stylisation.

Here, the line is continued from
the buttock to the heel. The
silhouette thus presents a hollow at
the back of the knee and at the
ankle.

Hollow.

Curve.

25

A few proportions

You don't need to take precise measurements of every part of the body to discover that you have drawn a leg too small or a head too big. Most of the time the your eye will tell you, even if you are a beginner.

The rules about how to calculate proportions are interesting, but, for me, they are not a useful approach to drawing the human body, particularly not when sketching, since slight variations in perspective can mess up everything. Nevertheless, here are a few rules concerning the long segments of the body.

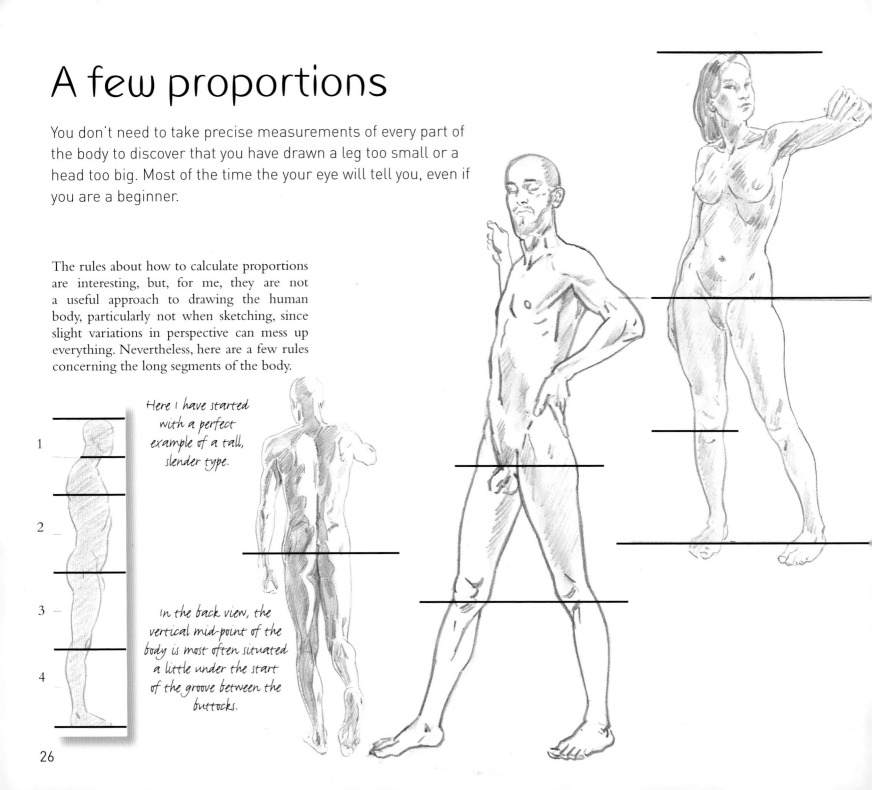

Here I have started with a perfect example of a tall, slender type.

In the back view, the vertical mid-point of the body is most often situated a little under the start of the groove between the buttocks.

1

2

3

4

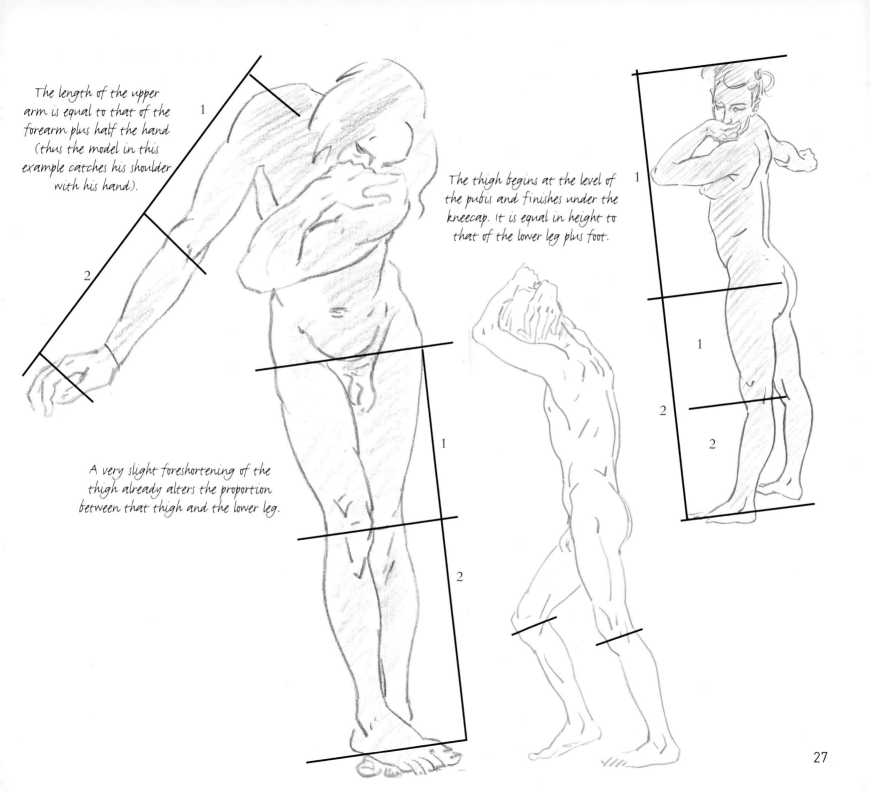

The length of the upper arm is equal to that of the forearm plus half the hand (thus the model in this example catches his shoulder with his hand).

1

2

The thigh begins at the level of the pubis and finishes under the kneecap. It is equal in height to that of the lower leg plus foot.

1

1

2

2

1

2

A very slight foreshortening of the thigh already alters the proportion between that thigh and the lower leg.

When the torso is straight,
the elbow is at the waist,
between the ribcage and
the pelvis. When the legs are
completely bent, the heels
come to the buttocks.

When the knee points outwards, the
heel comes to the crotch.

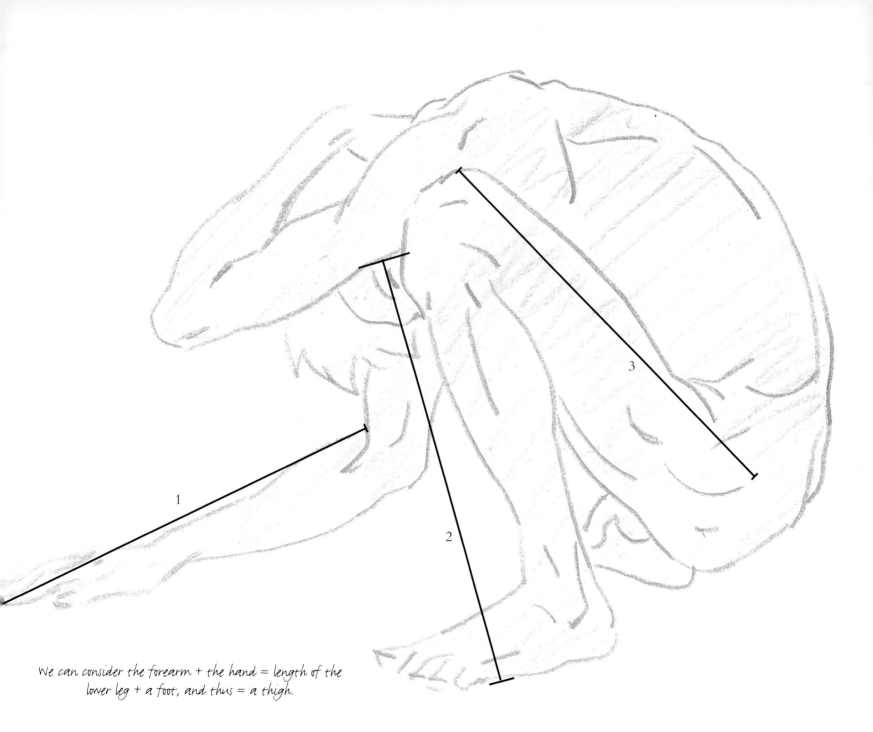

We can consider the forearm + the hand = length of the
lower leg + a foot, and thus = a thigh.

29

Differences in physical make-up between the sexes

Putting aside some proportions with regard to the skeleton, there are fatty areas that differentiate the male and female silhouettes, especially in the pelvic region.

It is the width of the pelvis, but above all the fatty deposits in this area, that strongly mark the difference in silhouette between the man and the woman. Here, the width of the shoulders is secondary.

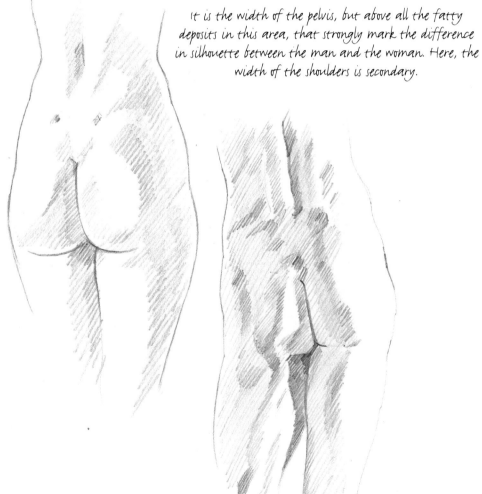

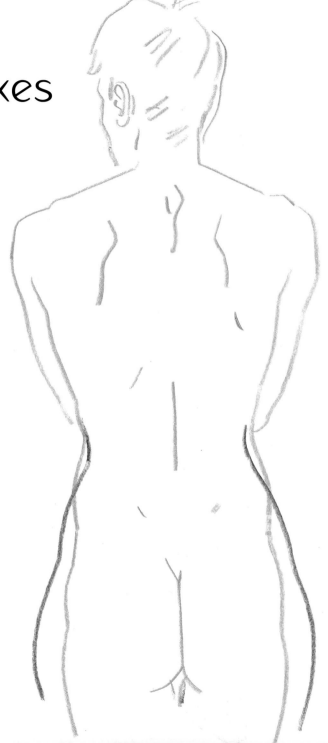

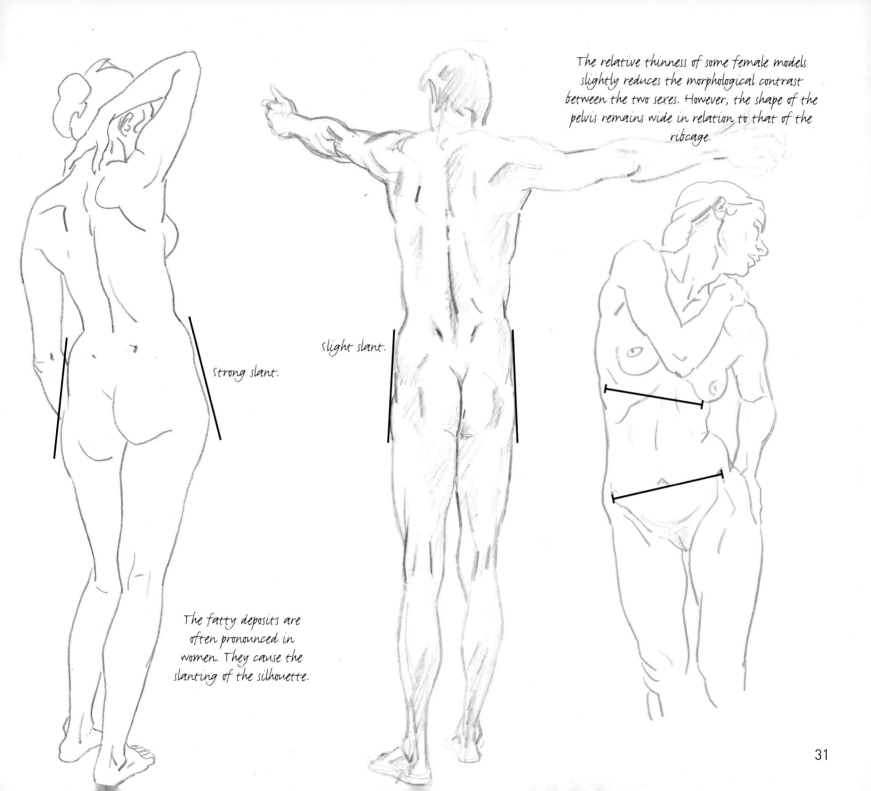

The relative thinness of some female models slightly reduces the morphological contrast between the two sexes. However, the shape of the pelvis remains wide in relation to that of the ribcage.

Strong slant.

slight slant.

The fatty deposits are often pronounced in women. They cause the slanting of the silhouette.

31

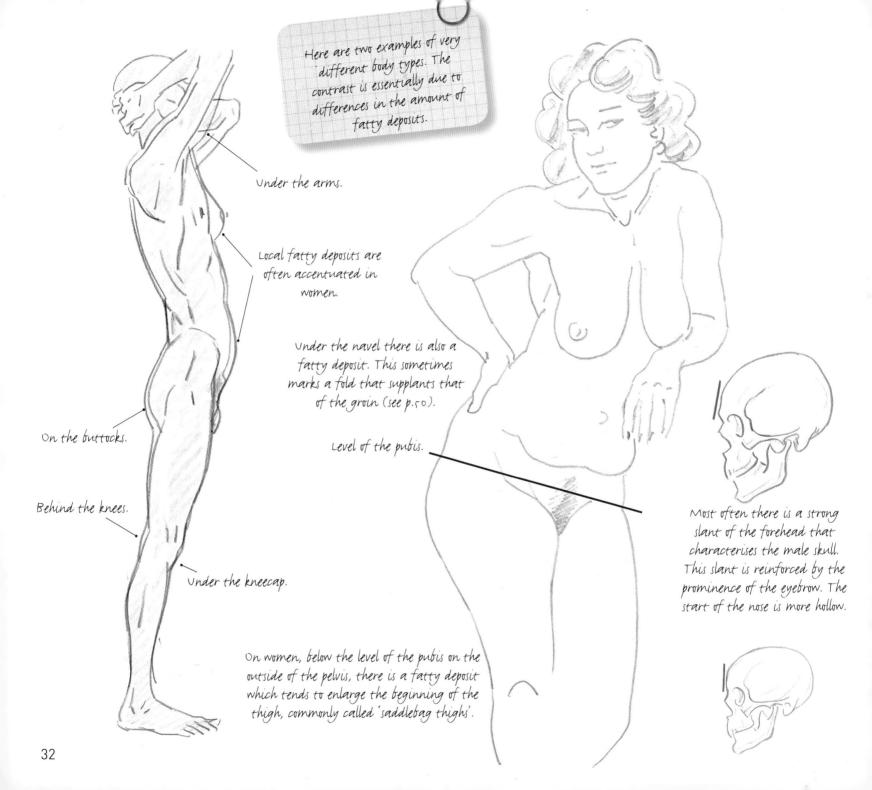

Under the arms.

Local fatty deposits are often accentuated in women.

Under the navel there is also a fatty deposit. This sometimes marks a fold that supplants that of the groin (see p.50).

On the buttocks.

Level of the pubis.

Behind the knees.

Under the kneecap.

Most often there is a strong slant of the forehead that characterises the male skull. This slant is reinforced by the prominence of the eyebrow. The start of the nose is more hollow.

On women, below the level of the pubis on the outside of the pelvis, there is a fatty deposit which tends to enlarge the beginning of the thigh, commonly called 'saddlebag thighs'.

rominence of
the eyebrow.

The bulge on the forehead
is generally more
accentuated in women.
The forehead appears to be
higher.

33

Skull, ribcage, pelvis: the three basic elements

These three elements are joined together by means of the vertebrae: the cervical vertebrae between the skull and the ribcage; and the lumbar vertebrae between the ribcage and the pelvis. The head is capable of a wide range of movements, supported by the first two cervical vertebrae. This results in some important imbalances between the skull and the ribcage.

Curves, twists and bends

The beauty of a pose often lies in the effects of the twists and turns between these three elements, and to the fact that none of them are facing in the same direction. To practise depicting such poses allows beginners to explore the spatial logic of drawing.

One could almost consider a posture simply by observing these three elements. Their disposition plays an important role in the dynamic of the pose.

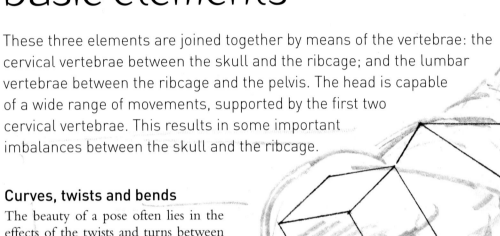

Changes of direction

Changes in direction can be found in many natural standing poses, especially when the figure is viewed in profile. A neck that bends the head forward, with the ribcage leaning in one direction and the pelvis in another, creates a dynamic pose.

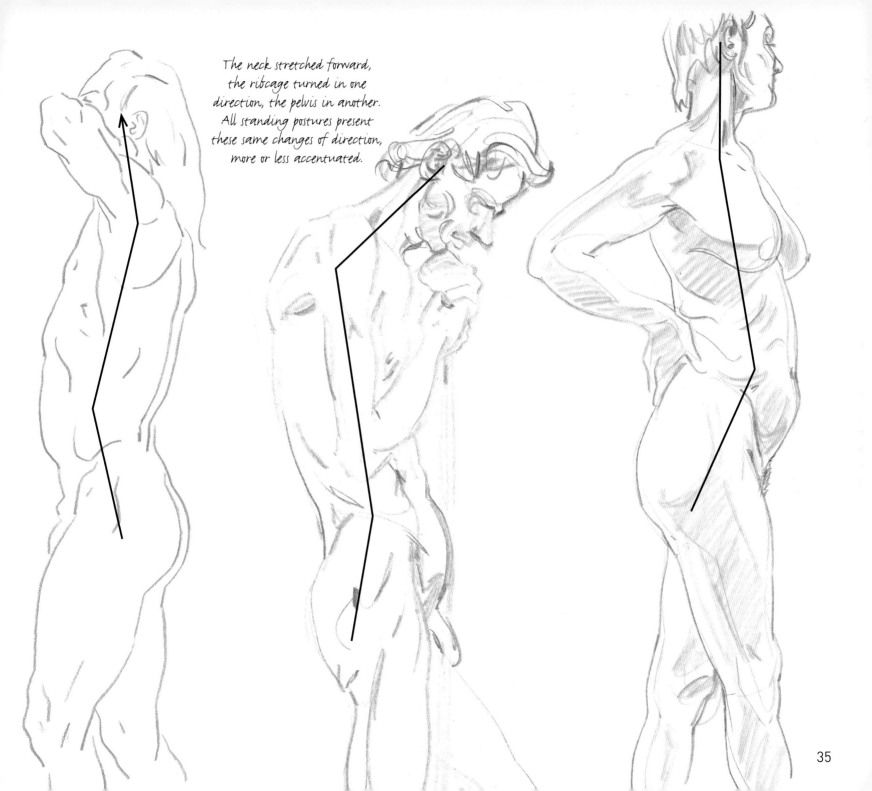

The neck stretched forward, the ribcage turned in one direction, the pelvis in another. All standing postures present these same changes of direction, more or less accentuated.

35

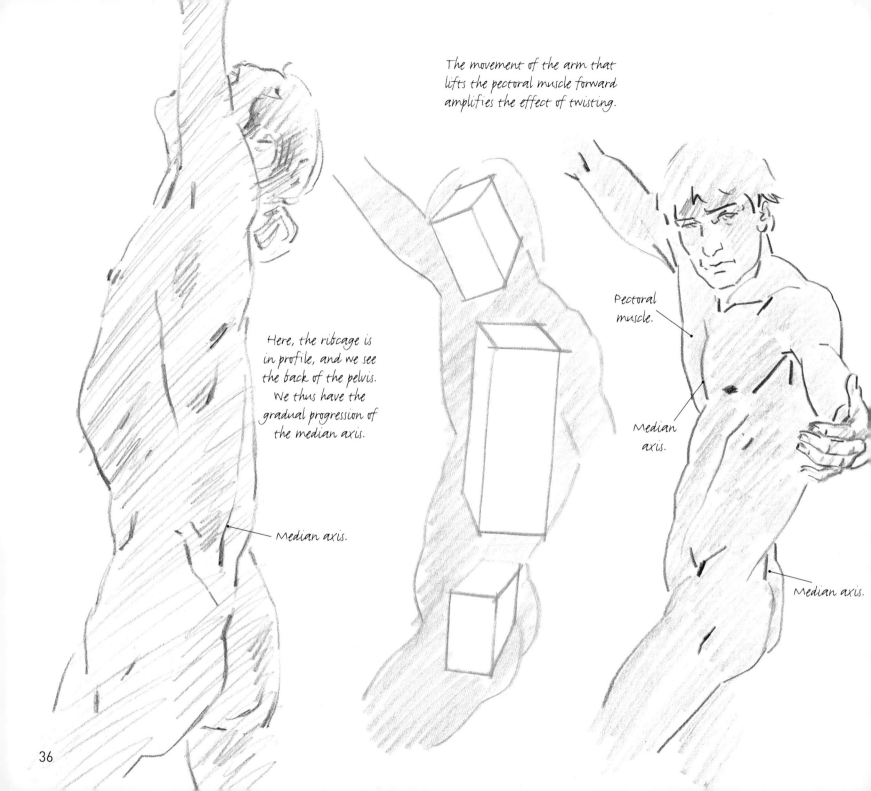

The movement of the arm that lifts the pectoral muscle forward amplifies the effect of twisting.

Here, the ribcage is in profile, and we see the back of the pelvis. We thus have the gradual progression of the median axis.

Median axis.

Pectoral muscle.

Median axis.

Median axis.

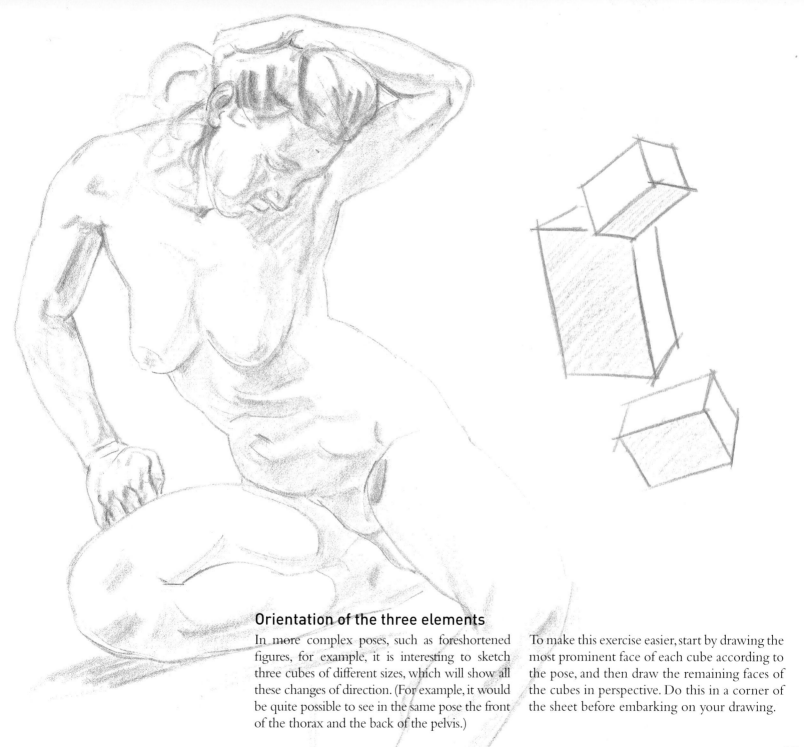

Orientation of the three elements

In more complex poses, such as foreshortened figures, for example, it is interesting to sketch three cubes of different sizes, which will show all these changes of direction. (For example, it would be quite possible to see in the same pose the front of the thorax and the back of the pelvis.)

To make this exercise easier, start by drawing the most prominent face of each cube according to the pose, and then draw the remaining faces of the cubes in perspective. Do this in a corner of the sheet before embarking on your drawing.

In this sketch I have chosen not to show the top part of the thorax to accentuate the contrast between the elements of the ribcage and the skull.

38

Here the twist is very impressive. The model is twisting around at the waist.

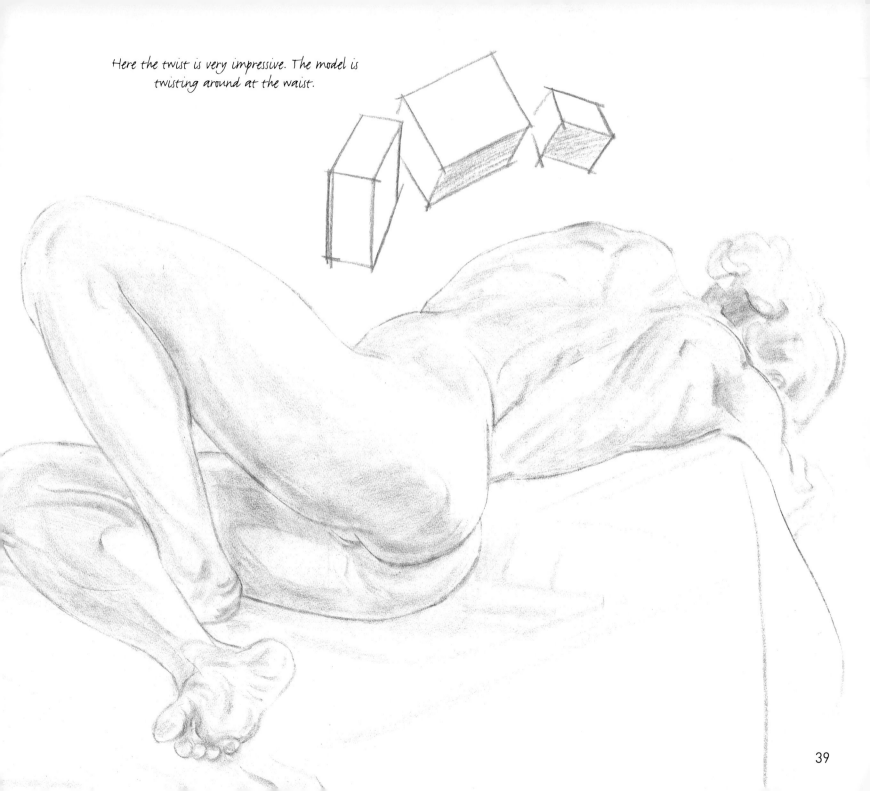

The torso

WHAT DOES HE NOT SEE IN THIS SECTION OF MAN THAT WE CALL THE TORSO? THE MUSCLES OF THE CHEST SWELL LIKE THE WAVES OF THE SEA; THE BROAD SHOULDERS, BENT, ARE A GREAT CONCAVE VAULT THAT DOES NOT BREAK, BUT ON THE CONTRARY, IS STRENGTHENED BY THE BURDEN IT IS WEIGHED DOWN WITH.

DIDEROT

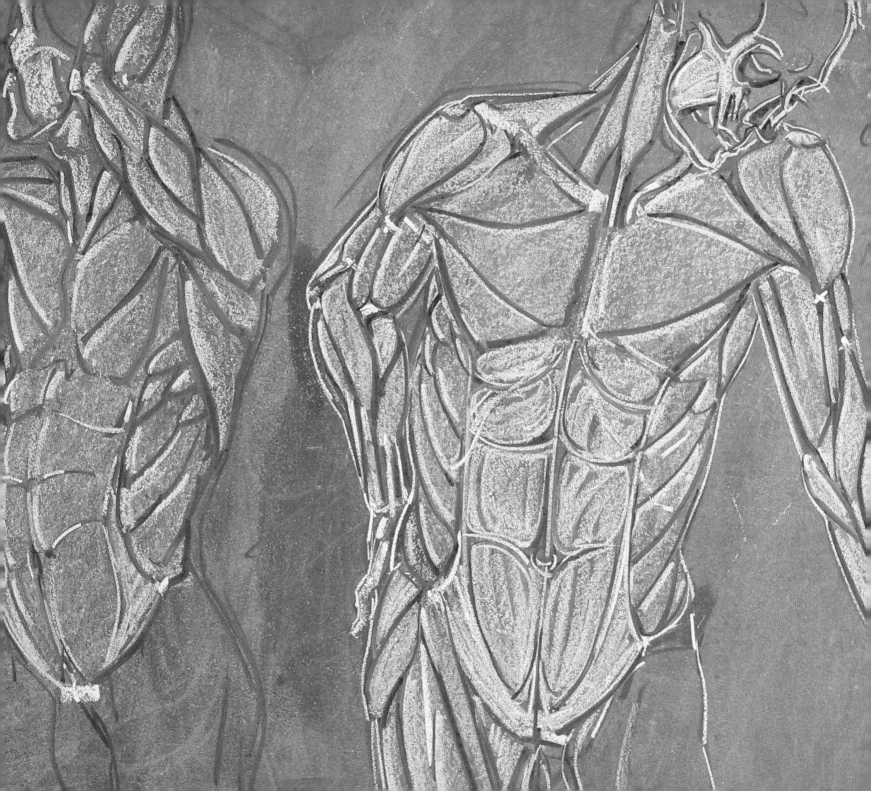

Organisation of the main curves

There is a graphic organisation that is more or less common to all bodies. Only extreme physical types (extremely thin or very obese) will deviate from these rules. We can therefore say that there is a graphic alphabet to consider – to ignore it is like making spelling mistakes.

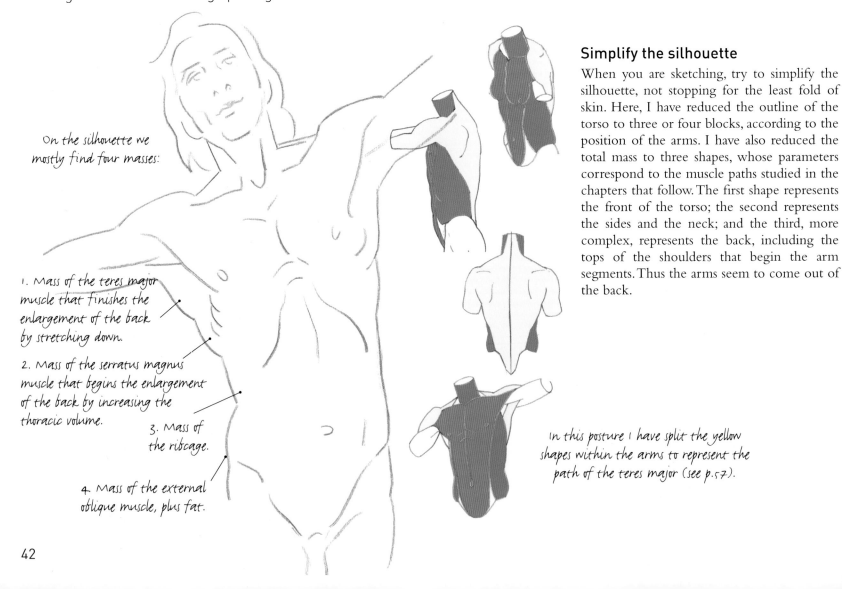

On the silhouette we mostly find four masses:

1. Mass of the teres major muscle that finishes the enlargement of the back by stretching down.

2. Mass of the serratus magnus muscle that begins the enlargement of the back by increasing the thoracic volume.

3. Mass of the ribcage.

4. Mass of the external oblique muscle, plus fat.

Simplify the silhouette

When you are sketching, try to simplify the silhouette, not stopping for the least fold of skin. Here, I have reduced the outline of the torso to three or four blocks, according to the position of the arms. I have also reduced the total mass to three shapes, whose parameters correspond to the muscle paths studied in the chapters that follow. The first shape represents the front of the torso; the second represents the sides and the neck; and the third, more complex, represents the back, including the tops of the shoulders that begin the arm segments. Thus the arms seem to come out of the back.

In this posture I have split the yellow shapes within the arms to represent the path of the teres major (see p.57).

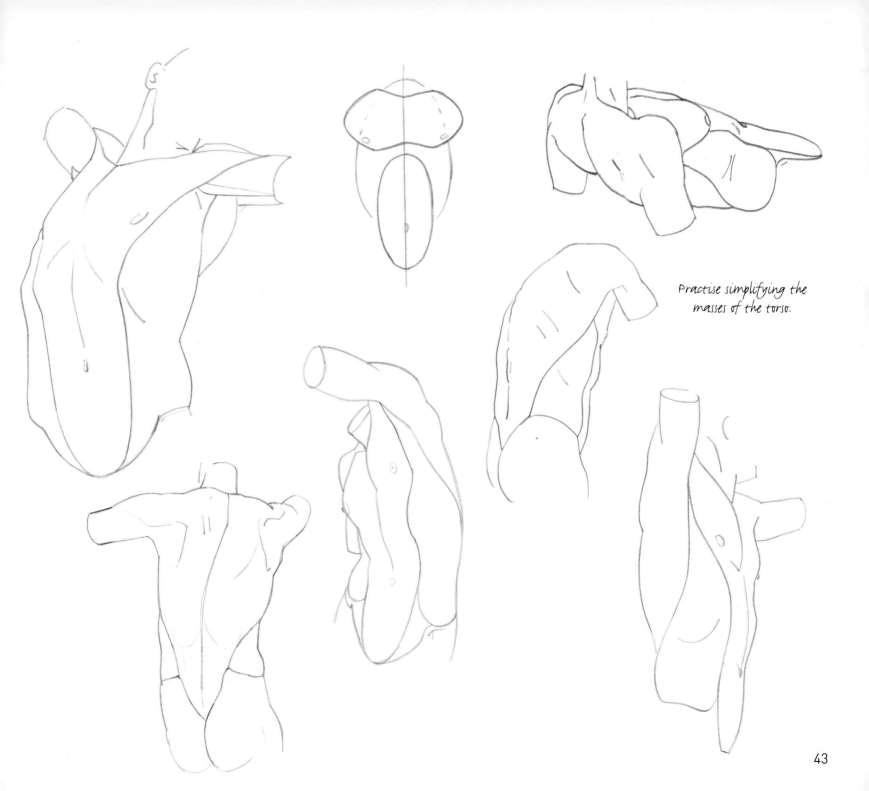

Practise simplifying the masses of the torso.

The torso from the front

The shapes that reveal the skeleton vary according to the different areas of the body; we can observe ridges, hollows, blocks or, again, linear paths. The bones are as important to represent graphically as are the muscles and tendons.

Look for the collarbone

The collarbone is almost entirely visible under the skin. It begins at the base of the neck where it is joined to the ribcage. Starting more or less on the horizontal, each end makes a wide curve along two thirds of its length, which allows it to reach round to the back without reducing the volume of the neck. The last third of each end begins the shape of the shoulders.

The general shape of the collarbone is like handlebars, with the last third being the handle, the end often forming a point above the shoulders. Each end appears totally independent of the other, and accompanies the arm movements.

These are views from above or below that reveal the true curvature of the collarbone, since viewed face-on it often looks like two straight lines.

The trapezius muscle stops at the collarbone, where the shoulder muscle starts, creating a graphic continuity that runs from the base of the skull at the back, to the arms in front.

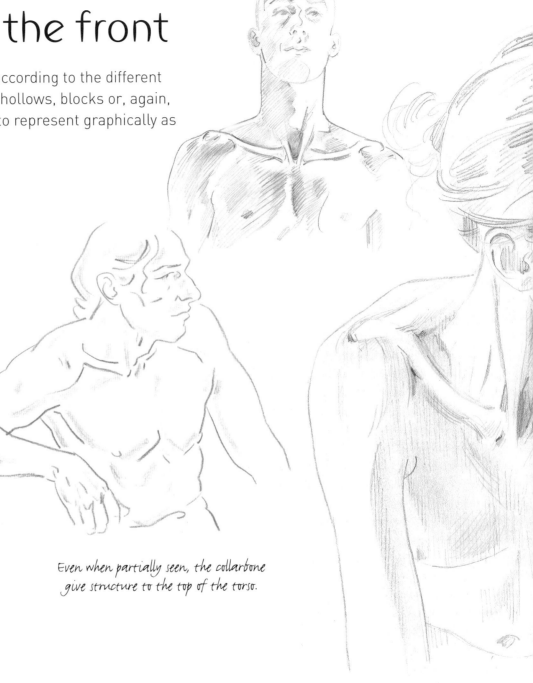

Even when partially seen, the collarbone give structure to the top of the torso.

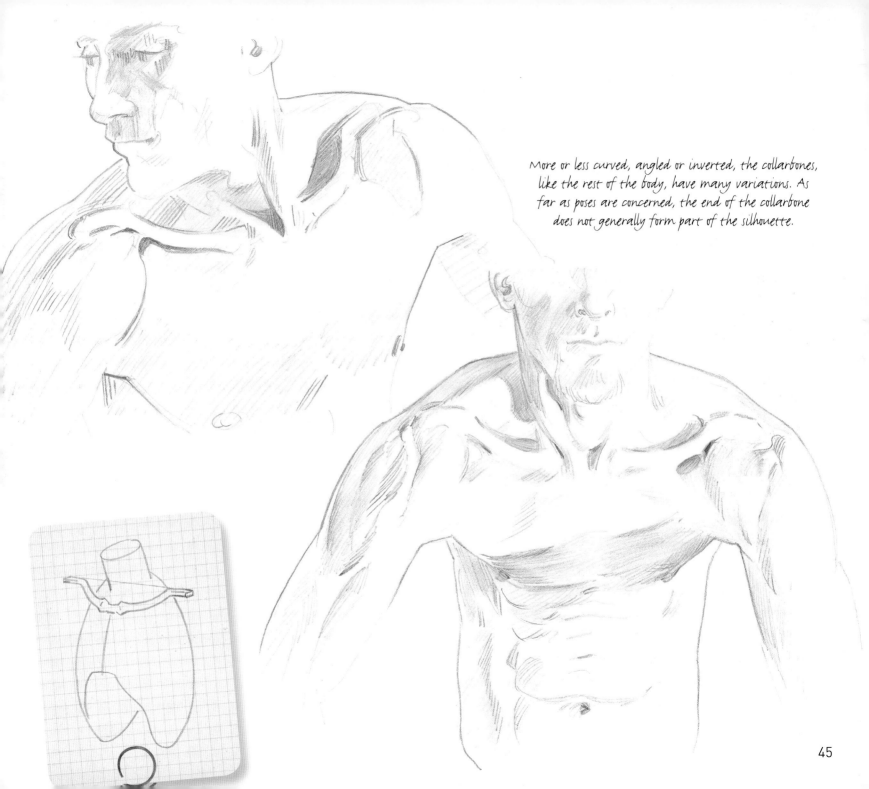

More or less curved, angled or inverted, the collarbones,
like the rest of the body, have many variations. As
far as poses are concerned, the end of the collarbone
does not generally form part of the silhouette.

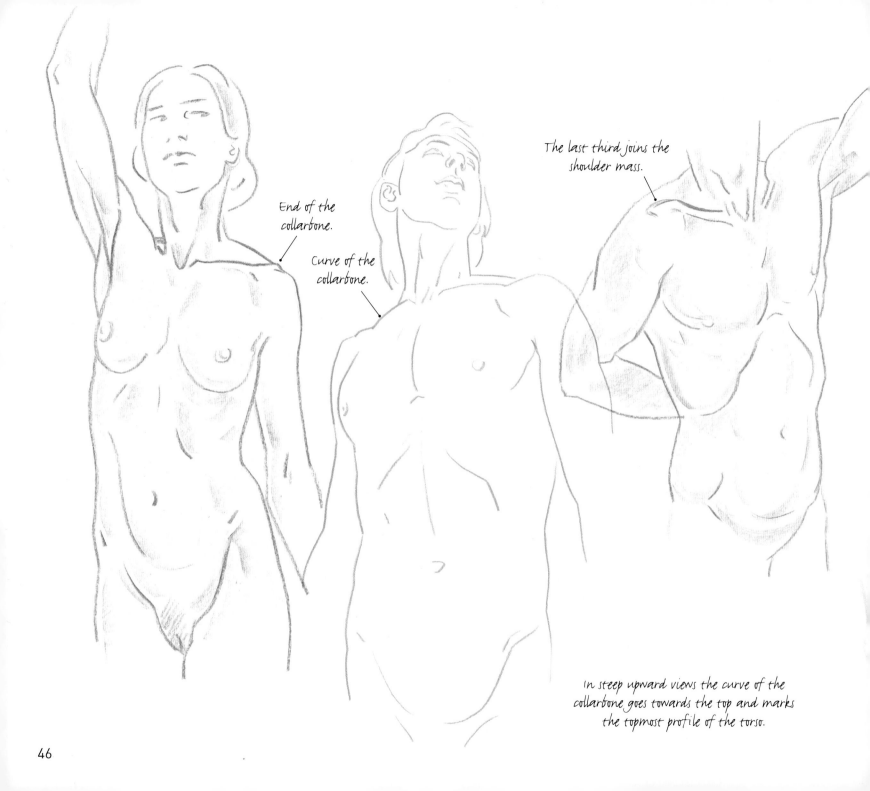

End of the
collarbone.

Curve of the
collarbone.

The last third joins the
shoulder mass.

In steep upward views the curve of the
collarbone goes towards the top and marks
the topmost profile of the torso.

There is no point looking for the collarbone when the arms are raised, as the pectoral muscle hides it with this movement.

Pectoral muscle.

A few structural points face-on

It is very useful to identify the base of the neck, the areolas, the navel and the anterior superior of the iliac spine. In fact, the exact placing of these points on the underlying mass is indispensable for a good depiction of the torso.

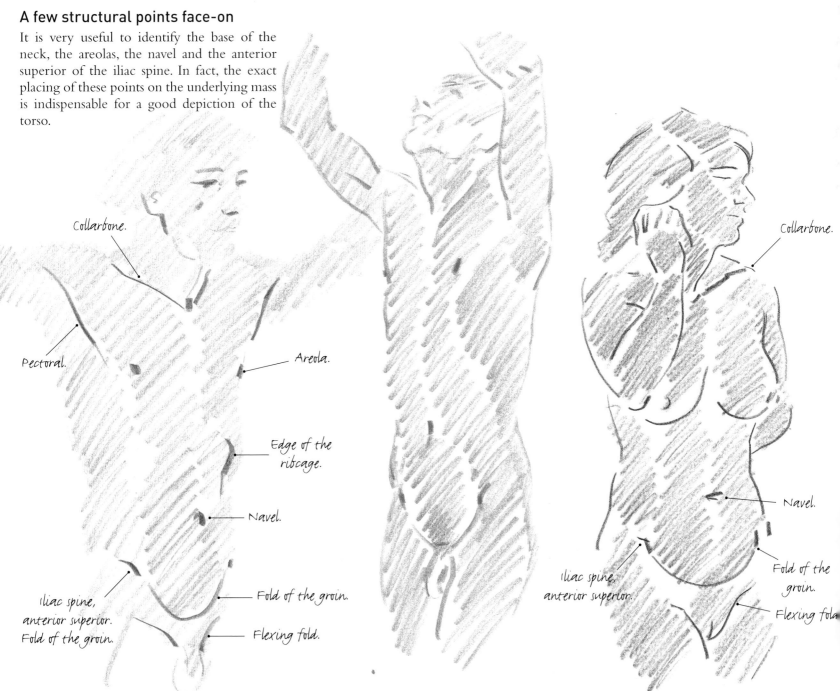

Collarbone.

Pectoral.

Areola.

Edge of the ribcage.

Navel.

Fold of the groin.

Iliac spine, anterior superior.
Fold of the groin.

Flexing fold.

Collarbone.

Navel.

Iliac spine, anterior superior.

Fold of the groin.

Flexing fold

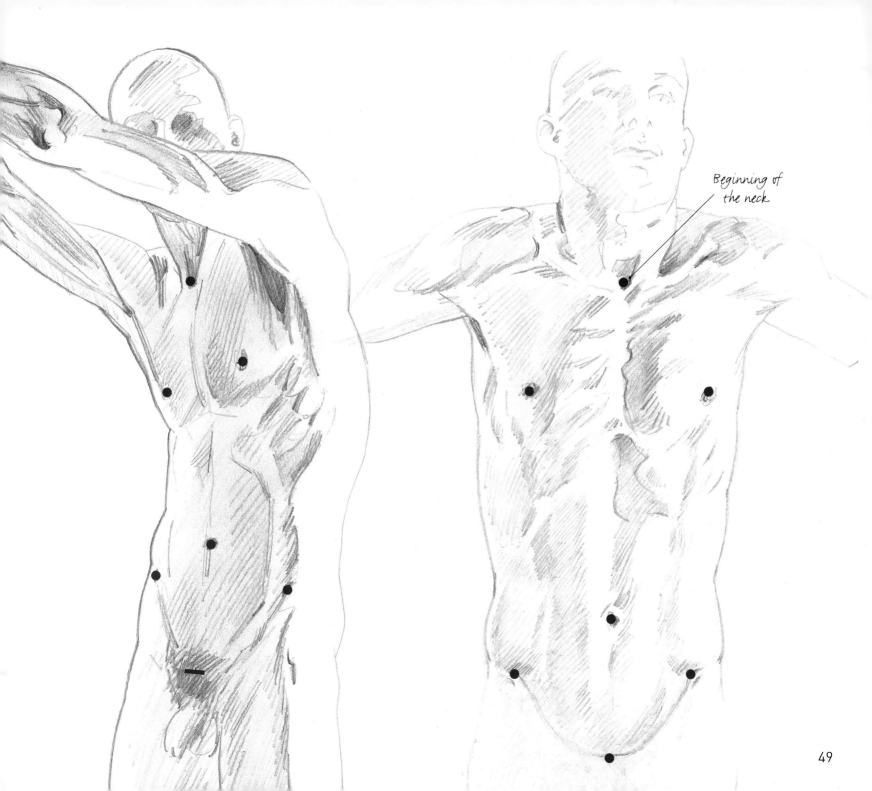

Beginning of
the neck.

49

The anterior iliac spine and the fold of the groin

At the front of the body, almost describing the breadth of the pelvis, two bony crests provide a point of contact for a tendon which joins them to the pubic bone (situated above the genitals). This tendon, which marks the fold of the groin, creates the frontal division between the torso and the lower limbs.

The narrower masculine pelvis leads into a tighter fold at the groin. The join with the pubic bone is hidden by the pubic hair. The genitals, suspended from the pubic bone, are therefore below the fold of the groin.

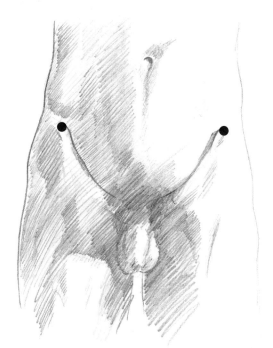

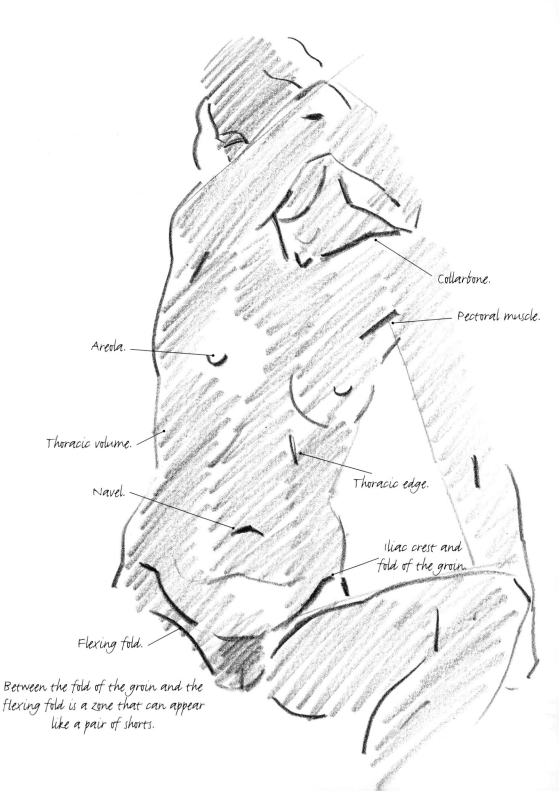

Collarbone.

Pectoral muscle.

Areola.

Thoracic volume.

Thoracic edge.

Navel.

Iliac crest and fold of the groin.

Flexing fold.

Between the fold of the groin and the flexing fold is a zone that can appear like a pair of shorts.

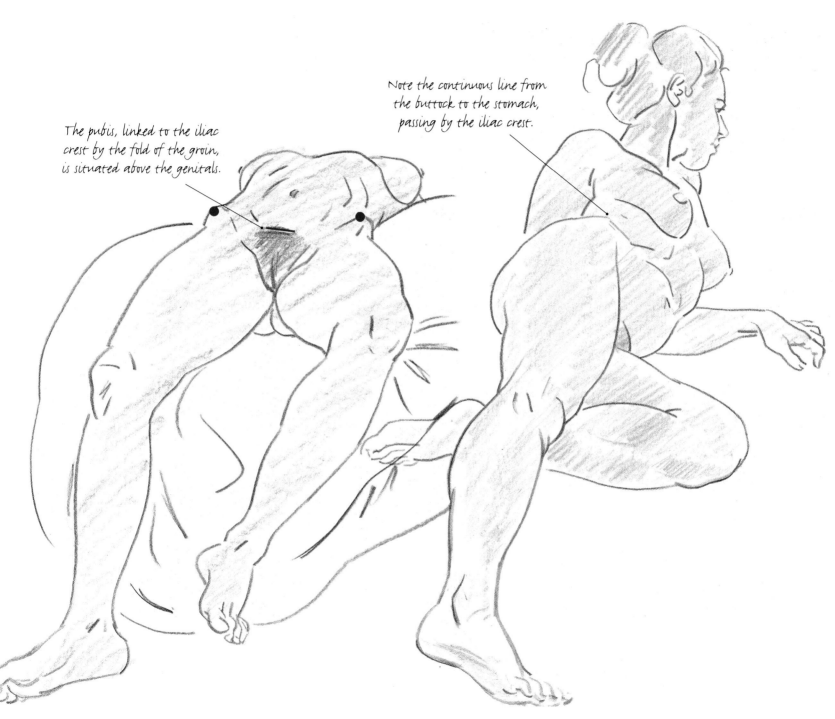

The pubis, linked to the iliac crest by the fold of the groin, is situated above the genitals.

Note the continuous line from the buttock to the stomach, passing by the iliac crest.

51

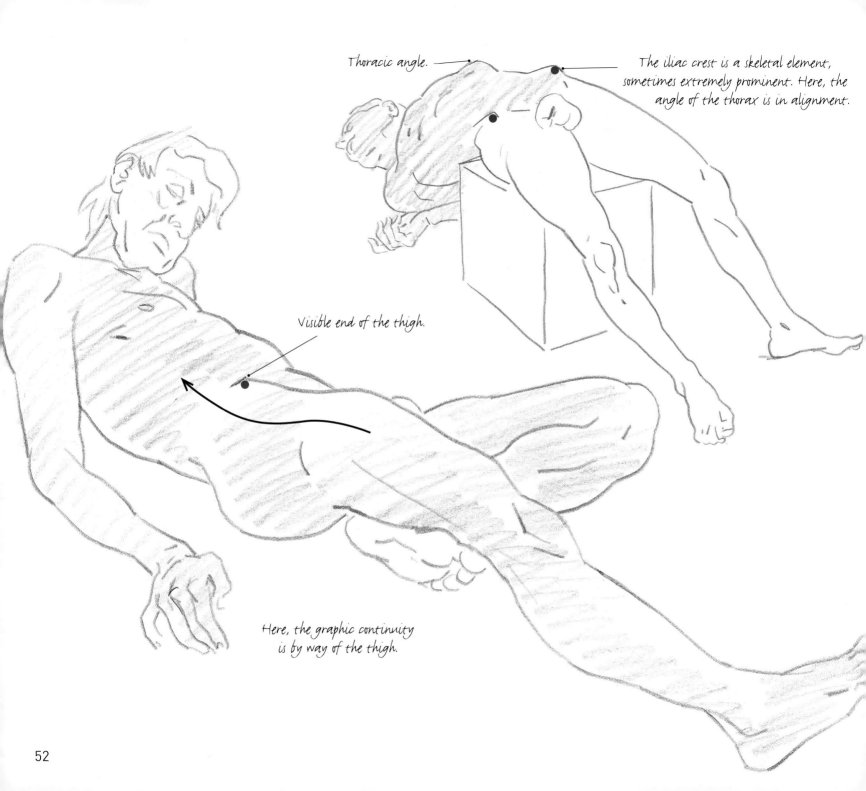

Thoracic angle.

The iliac crest is a skeletal element, sometimes extremely prominent. Here, the angle of the thorax is in alignment.

Visible end of the thigh.

Here, the graphic continuity is by way of the thigh.

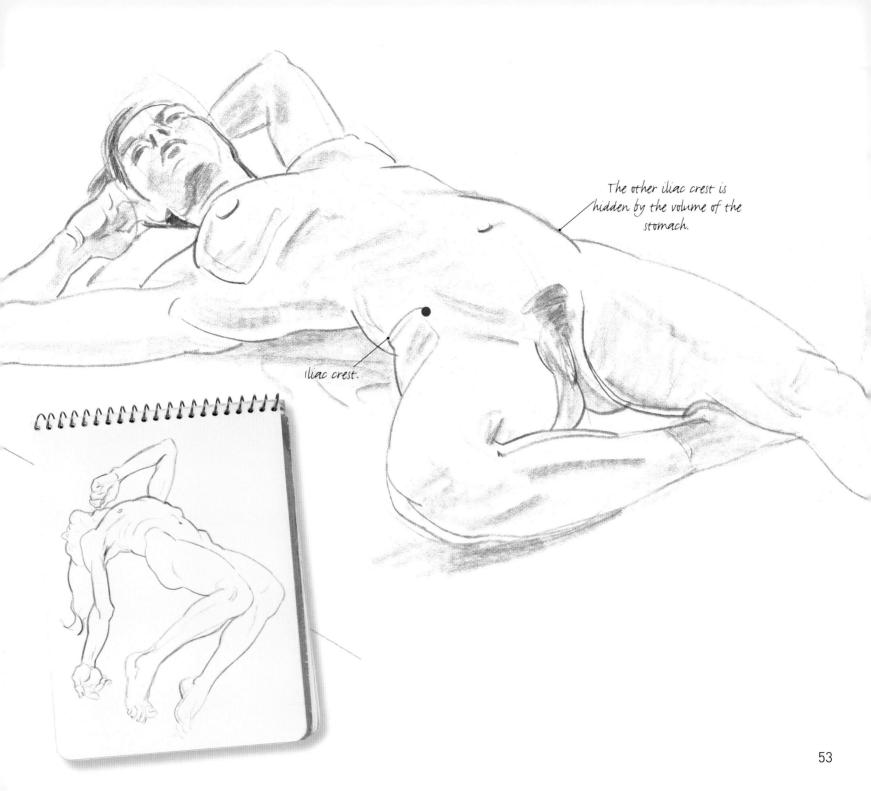

The other iliac crest is hidden by the volume of the stomach.

Iliac crest.

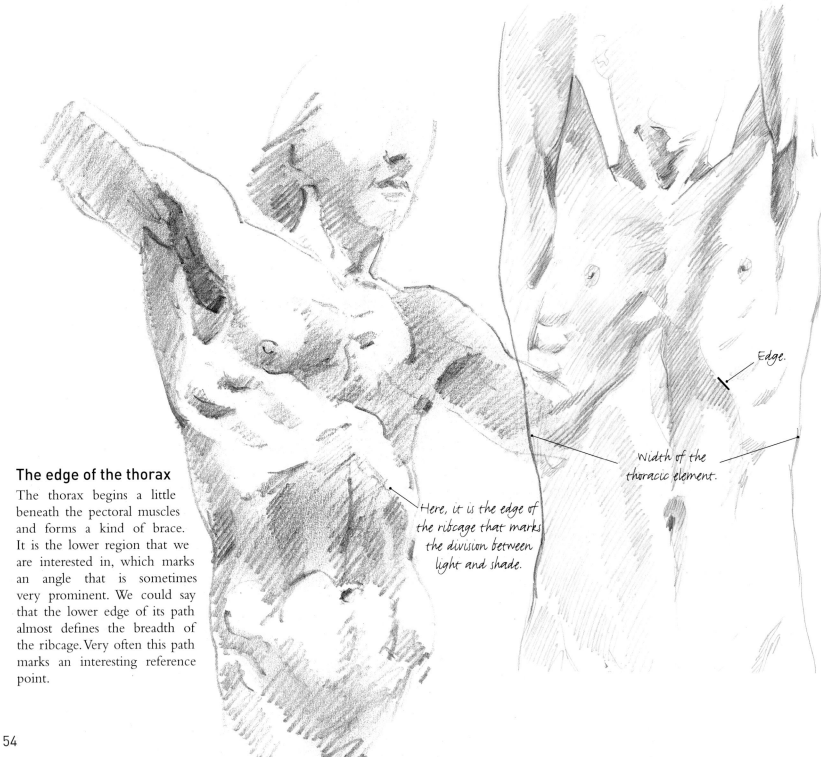

The edge of the thorax

The thorax begins a little beneath the pectoral muscles and forms a kind of brace. It is the lower region that we are interested in, which marks an angle that is sometimes very prominent. We could say that the lower edge of its path almost defines the breadth of the ribcage. Very often this path marks an interesting reference point.

Here, it is the edge of the ribcage that marks the division between light and shade.

Edge.

Width of the thoracic element.

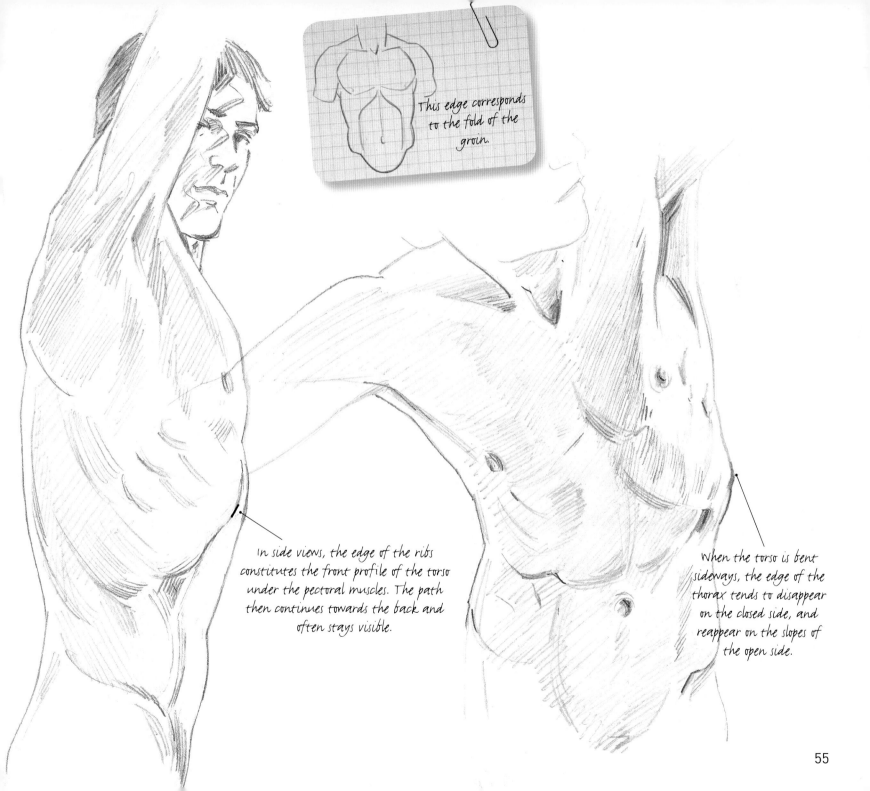

This edge corresponds to the fold of the groin.

In side views, the edge of the ribs constitutes the front profile of the torso under the pectoral muscles. The path then continues towards the back and often stays visible.

When the torso is bent sideways, the edge of the thorax tends to disappear on the closed side, and reappear on the slopes of the open side.

55

Pectoral and abdominal muscles: a large apron

The pectoral muscle is enormous, occupying the larger part of the thorax at the front of the body. It moves outwards, rolling around the arms and passing under the shoulder muscle, marking a graphic link. The base is of equal width, and joins the abdominal muscles, which are situated below, and themselves join the pubis. The result is a continuity corresponding to the sides of these muscles, reaching from the arms as far as the pelvis, and covering the full height of the torso. In other words, we can consider that these two muscles occupy the whole front of the torso.

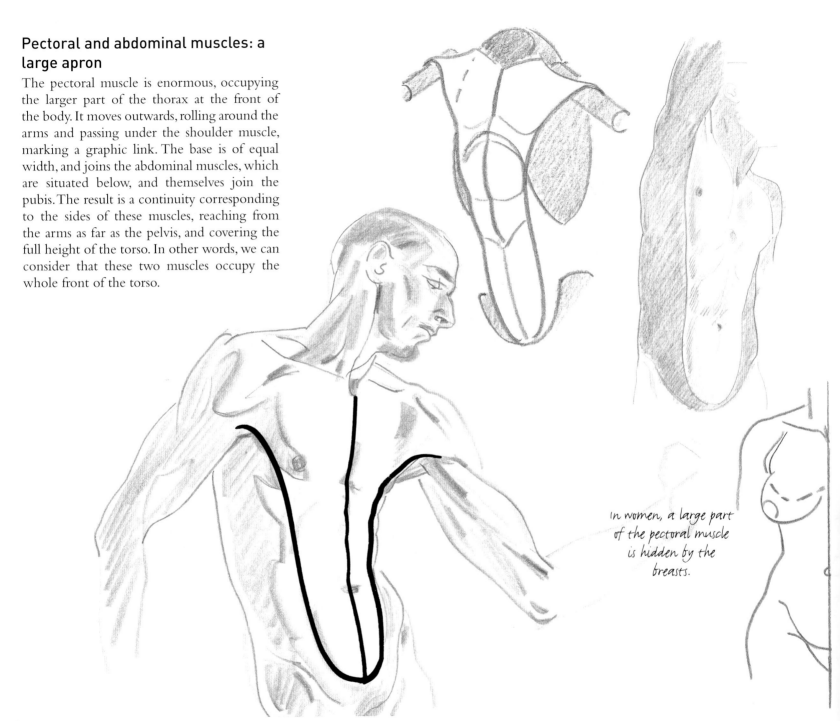

In women, a large part of the pectoral muscle is hidden by the breasts.

56

The pectoral and teres major muscles: an eventual continuity

The teres major muscle, which starts at the base of the shoulder blade, climbs towards the inside face of the arm which it perforates, thus dividing it in two. It delineates the bottom edge of the armpit hollow. We can easily imagine a continuity with the pectoral muscle passing across the arms (see pp.65 and 72).

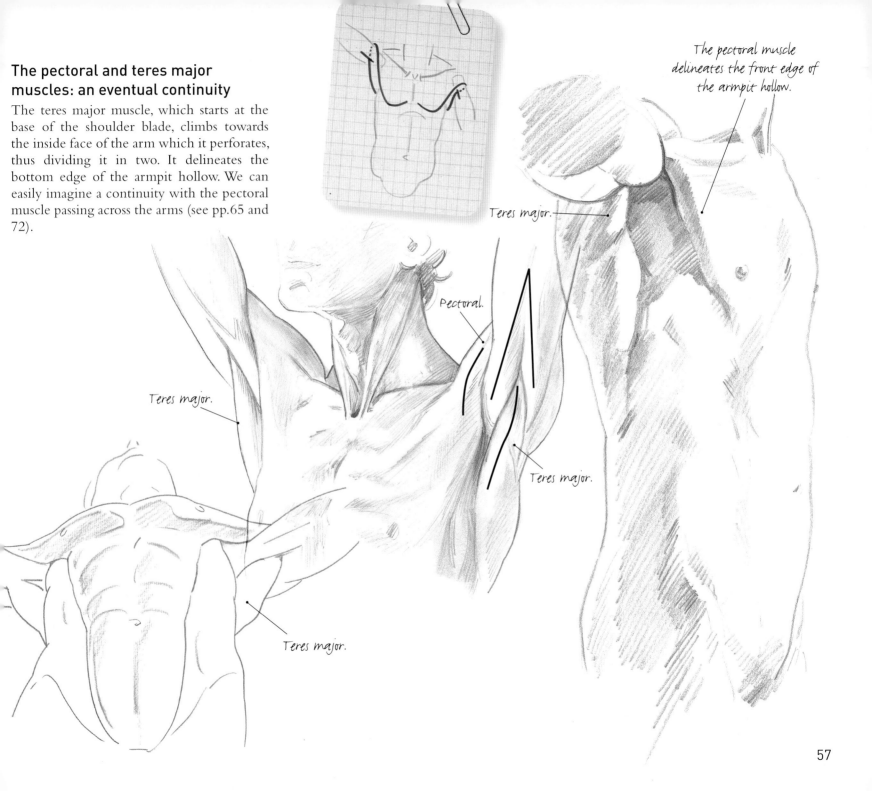

The pectoral muscle delineates the front edge of the armpit hollow.

Teres major.

Teres major.

Pectoral.

Teres major.

Teres major.

The back torso

When we look at the back we can observe a median axis from the base of the skull to the buttocks. This is hollow or in relief, depending on the area and body movements.

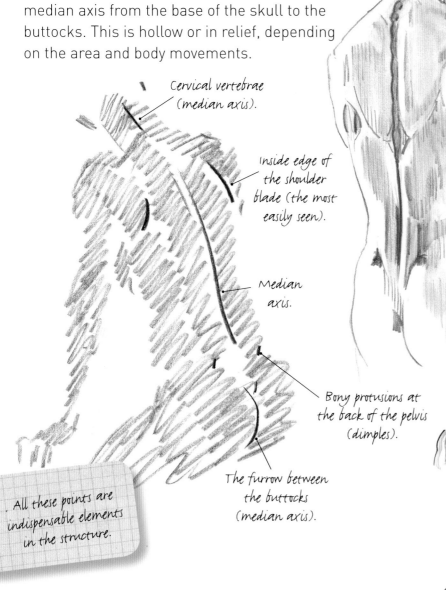

Cervical vertebrae (median axis).

Inside edge of the shoulder blade (the most easily seen).

Median axis.

Bony protusions at the back of the pelvis (dimples).

The furrow between the buttocks (median axis).

All these points are indispensable elements in the structure.

A median axis, the spinal vertebrae and/or furrows

At the back of the neck, whatever the movements of the head, we often see a furrow created by the muscles. Gradually, as we look down, the bones of the spine clearly appear. The last cervical bone, the seventh, very prominent, marks the base of the neck and the summit of the thorax mass. The bones of the vertebral column are easily seen down to the base of the back where they are again swallowed up by two columns of large muscles down to the pelvis. In some movements, when the torso is flexed towards the front, we can nevertheless see them again. Following this path with the furrow between the buttocks, we see a median axis which is very useful when deciding the orientation of the three main elements (see p.34).

The same bony element can appear in two forms: a knob or a hollow. All depends on the physical make-up of the subject and/or the posture. The best examples of this are the bones at the back of the pelvis. The skin is fastened on to these two bony reference points, which are rather pointed. In a model with a thin body shape we can clearly see these bones under the skin. With a plumper model, there is fat all around this area, except for these two points of adherence of the skin which thus appear as fasteners, forming dimples. Apart from extreme differences in morphology, these are the dimples that we most often see when the model is standing.

The median axis of the back
presents a series of small ridges
that are clearly seen at the
thorax level.

When the shoulder blades move towards the
front, they reveal the bulk of the thorax,
which itself presents the retracting angle
of the ribs, thus creating a large furrow
where the dorsal spine lies.

Retracting angle.

Median axis.

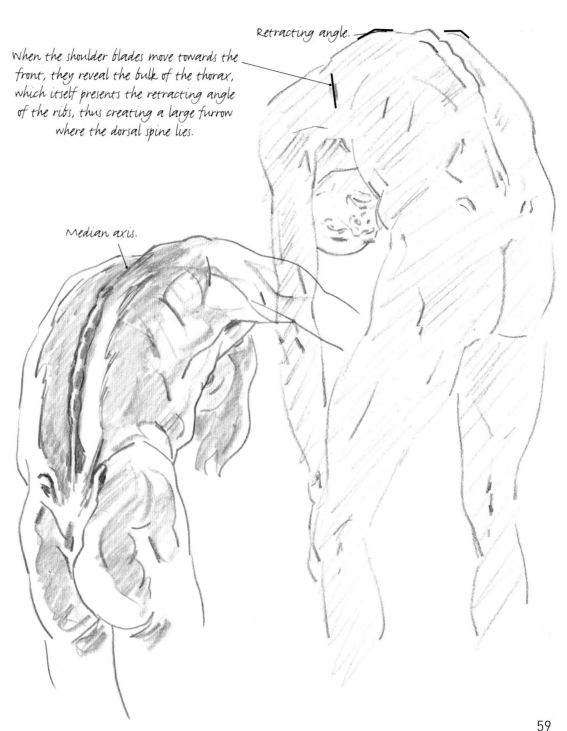

This median axis can be distorted by
movement of the shoulders, in this case
going in the opposite direction to the
three-quarters view shown.

59

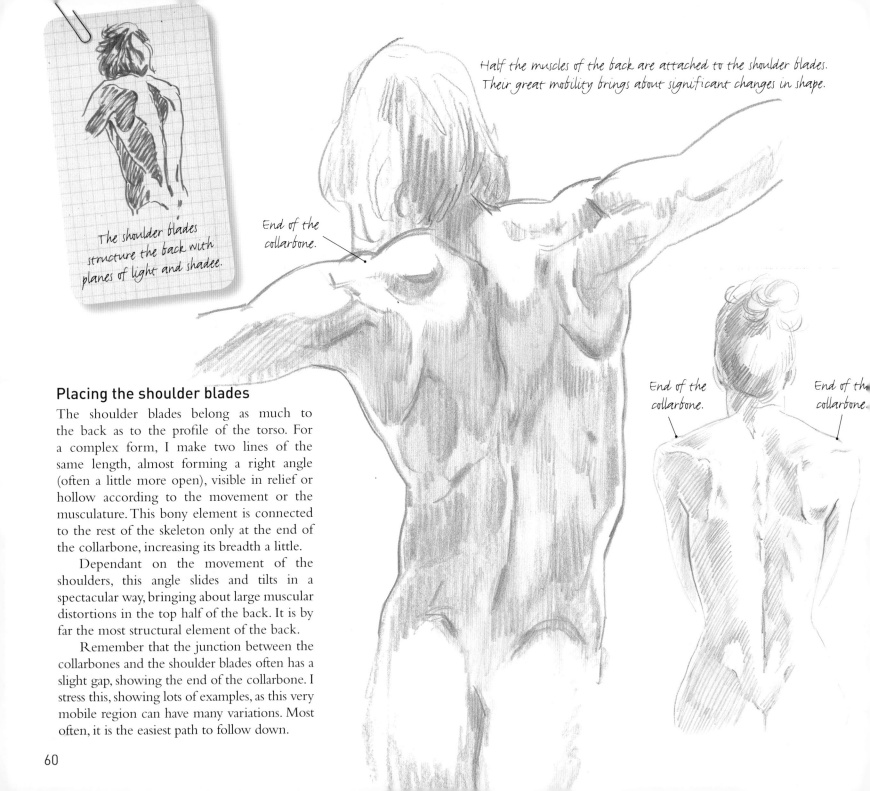

The shoulder blades structure the back with planes of light and shadee.

Half the muscles of the back are attached to the shoulder blades. Their great mobility brings about significant changes in shape.

End of the collarbone.

End of the collarbone.

End of the collarbone.

Placing the shoulder blades

The shoulder blades belong as much to the back as to the profile of the torso. For a complex form, I make two lines of the same length, almost forming a right angle (often a little more open), visible in relief or hollow according to the movement or the musculature. This bony element is connected to the rest of the skeleton only at the end of the collarbone, increasing its breadth a little.

Dependant on the movement of the shoulders, this angle slides and tilts in a spectacular way, bringing about large muscular distortions in the top half of the back. It is by far the most structural element of the back.

Remember that the junction between the collarbones and the shoulder blades often has a slight gap, showing the end of the collarbone. I stress this, showing lots of examples, as this very mobile region can have many variations. Most often, it is the easiest path to follow down.

Lifting the shoulder
accentuates the tilt of
the shoulder blade.

When the arms are
lifted up high the point
of the shoulder blade
moves towards the side.

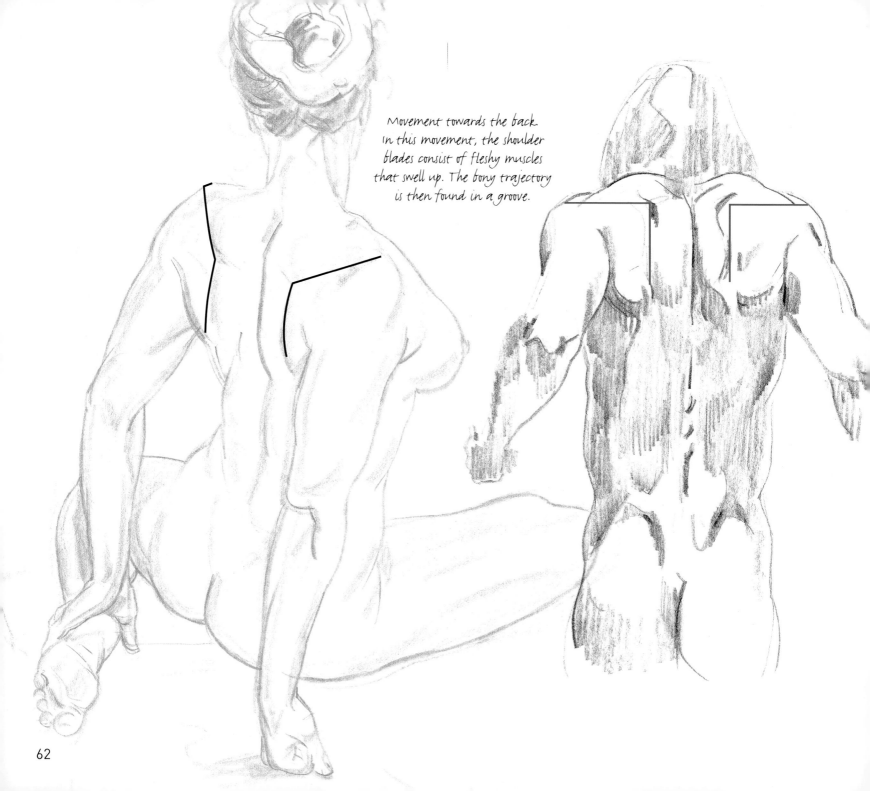

Movement towards the back.
In this movement, the shoulder
blades consist of fleshy muscles
that swell up. The bony trajectory
is then found in a groove.

Movement towards the front. This movement of the shoulders towards the front stretches the back muscles, showing the bulk of the thorax and the dorsal vertebrae.

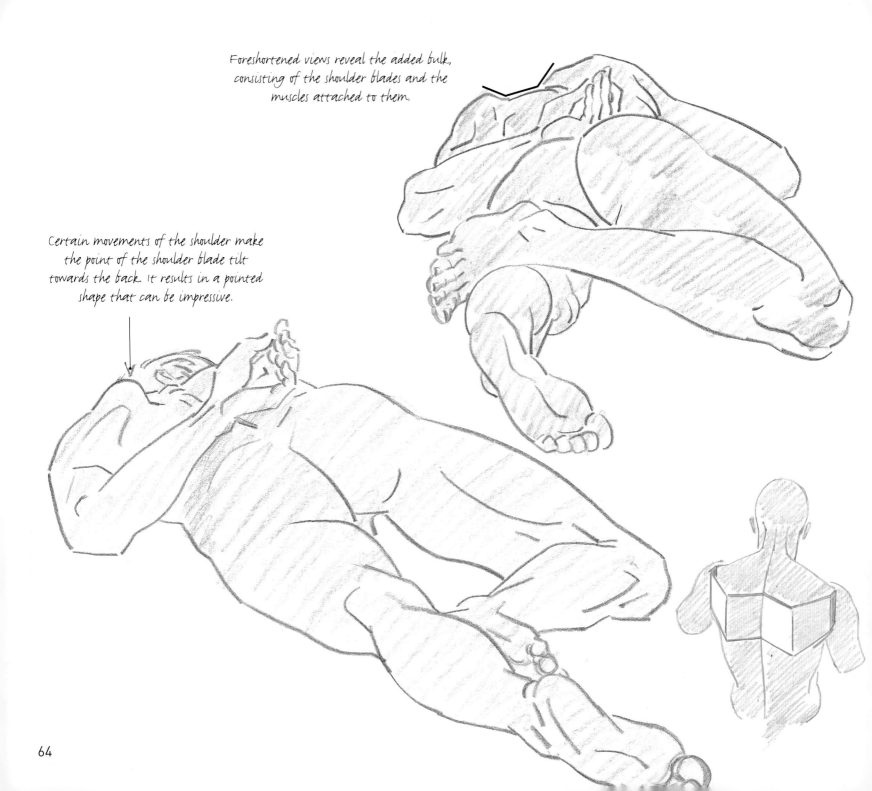

Foreshortened views reveal the added bulk,
consisting of the shoulder blades and the
muscles attached to them.

Certain movements of the shoulder make
the point of the shoulder blade tilt
towards the back. It results in a pointed
shape that can be impressive.

64

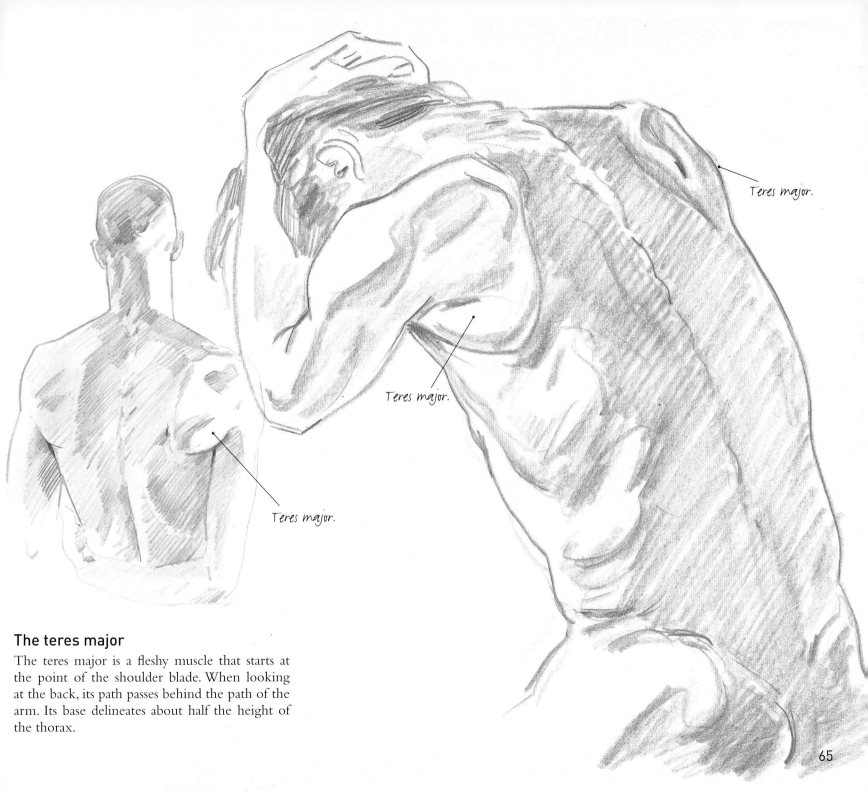

Teres major.

Teres major.

Teres major.

The teres major

The teres major is a fleshy muscle that starts at the point of the shoulder blade. When looking at the back, its path passes behind the path of the arm. Its base delineates about half the height of the thorax.

65

Plates of tendons with geometric shapes

The trapezius muscle is attached to the spine and the shoulder blades by triangular and diamond-shaped tendons. These elements, which have little or no bulk of their own, reveal the underlying bulk of the muscles.

The trapezius muscle

The trapezius is a fleshy muscle, connected to plates of tendons. The tendons form structured shapes that become clearer when the trapezius muscle is contracted.

Plates of tendons (tendons attached to the trapezius muscle).

Trapezius muscle.

When the arms are lifted, the trapezius is contracted.

These shapes appear in contraction, pulled by the muscles surrounding them.

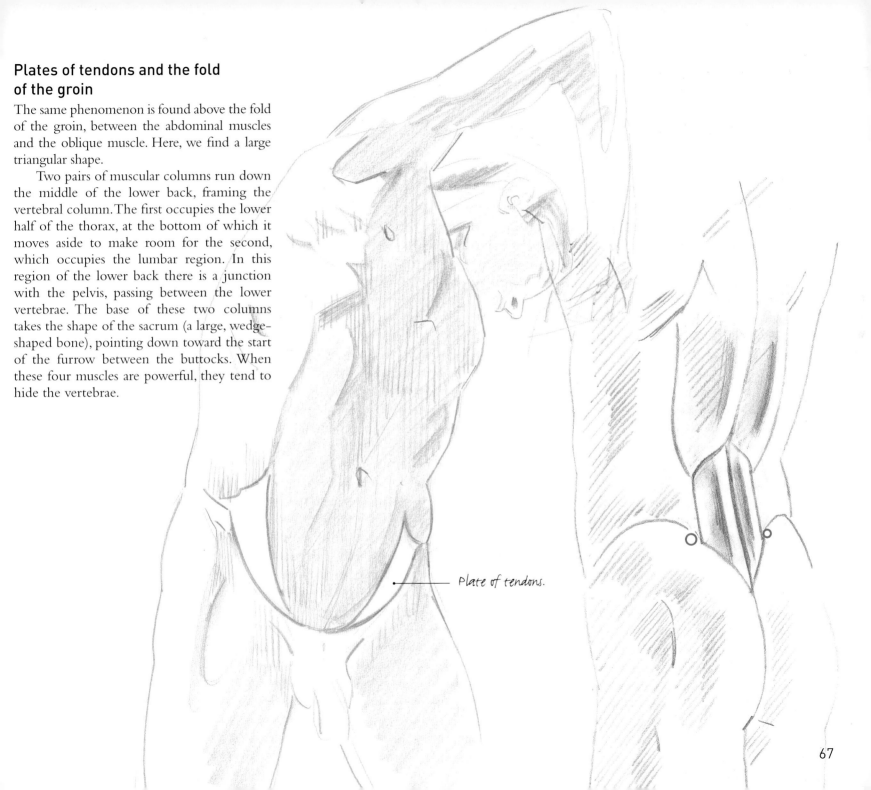

Plates of tendons and the fold of the groin

The same phenomenon is found above the fold of the groin, between the abdominal muscles and the oblique muscle. Here, we find a large triangular shape.

Two pairs of muscular columns run down the middle of the lower back, framing the vertebral column. The first occupies the lower half of the thorax, at the bottom of which it moves aside to make room for the second, which occupies the lumbar region. In this region of the lower back there is a junction with the pelvis, passing between the lower vertebrae. The base of these two columns takes the shape of the sacrum (a large, wedge-shaped bone), pointing down toward the start of the furrow between the buttocks. When these four muscles are powerful, they tend to hide the vertebrae.

Plate of tendons.

The neck

The bulk of the neck appears as a cylinder that projects the face towards the front. Put another way, its trajectory is in an upward direction and the face is thus found positioned in front of the shoulders. Let us consider that this is due to the fact that the base of the neck is itself attached to the top of the torso at an angle.

The sterno-cleido-mastoid

Like a flexible tube, the neck can turn in all directions, even making the skin fold like an accordion when it tilts back. Viewed face on, things are even simpler; the base is centred between the two shoulders and its bulk is straight. However, its final build is determined by a muscle that doesn't belong to it directly, but which is, however, easily the most remarkable element in the area: the sterno-cleido-mastoid.

When we turn our heads, this muscle can be seen all down its length. It starts from the skull, behind the ear, runs round the neck and is attached back and front at the base by two extremely graphic tendons that pass between the two collarbones. It also has a flatter branch that is attached directly to the collarbone.

When viewed in profile, its path lies in the opposite direction to the bulk of the neck, forming a cross. When the head is turned to the maximum, its insertion point into the skull clearly moves towards the front, cancelling its slant.

These two ribbons (sometimes wide) of the sterno-cleido-mastoid are attached to the top of the thorax by means of a tendon, much thinner, that passes beween the collarbones.

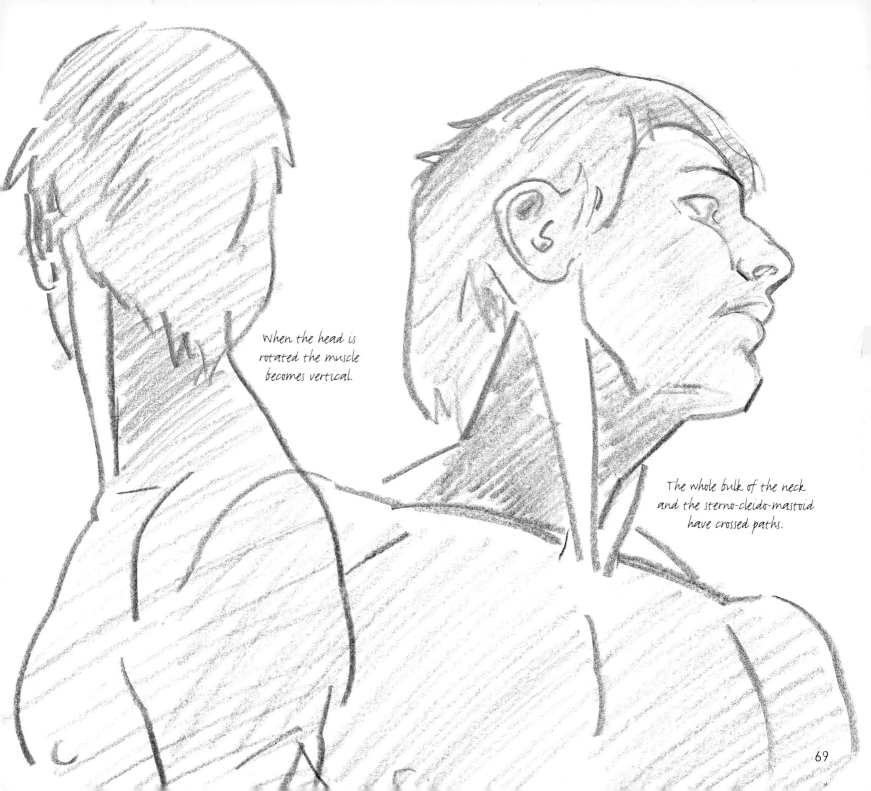

When the head is rotated the muscle becomes vertical.

The whole bulk of the neck and the sterno-cleido-mastoid have crossed paths.

The torso in profile

The shoulder is a block of bone, turned towards the front, to which is fixed the deltoid muscle. In this chapter we return to the elements of the body described face on and/or from the back. It is interesting to note that the two profiles are different.

A shoulder rounded in front

The arrangement of the arm bone at the level of the shoulder joint (which I will not describe here) means that it establishes, with the deltoid muscle, the form and build of the body. This arrangement makes the observation of profiles and views in perspective more interesting, where we notice a round mass completely turned towards the front. This mass extends beyond the collarbone and the shoulder blades, marking a contrast with the back silhouette, rendered almost flat by the shoulder blade and the muscles attached to it.

slight slope.

Mass of the top end of the arm bone.

slant of the thorax amplified by the pectoral muscle.

The shoulder mass is more or less rounded due to the presence of the bone, which is fixed to the frontal region of the deltoid muscle.

The arrangement of the top end of the arm bone (humerus) at the level of the shoulder, means that its mass extends in front of the end of the collarbone and the shoulder blade. It results in a shoulder that is rounded in front and flatter behind.

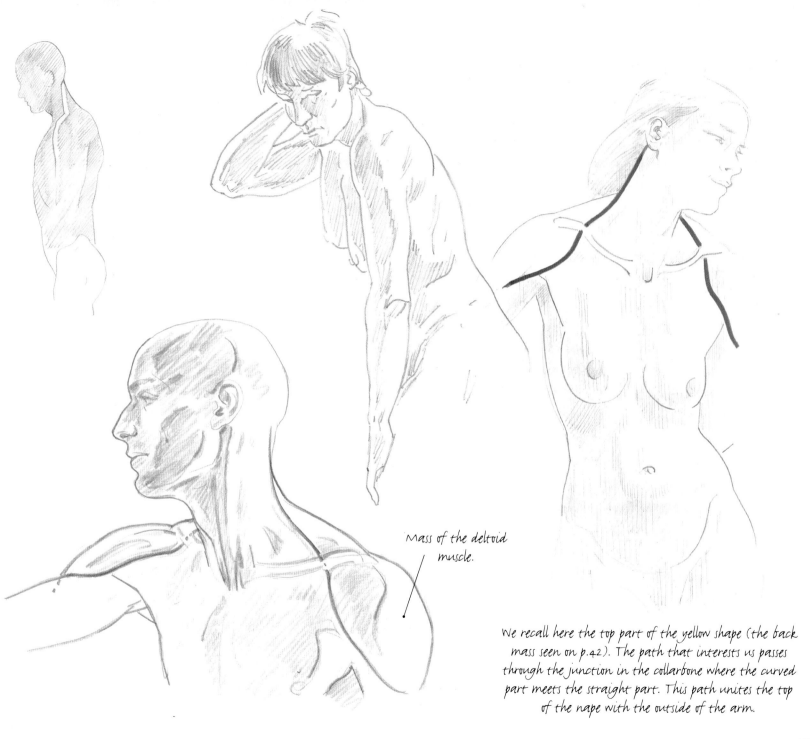

Mass of the deltoid
muscle.

We recall here the top part of the yellow shape (the back
mass seen on p.42). The path that interests us passes
through the junction in the collarbone where the curved
part meets the straight part. This path unites the top
of the nape with the outside of the arm.

The teres major and the latissimus dorsi

The large dorsal muscle (latissimus dorsi), unites the inside arm with the back of the pelvis, dividing the torso in two in profile.

Latissimus dorsi

When the arms move away from the torso, they reveal the side of the thorax. Here we can see the long path of a bundle of muscle fibres that join the inside of the arm, near the hollow of the armpit, with the back of the pelvis: this is the large dorsal muscle.

Dorsal vertebrae.

shoulder blade.

Teres major.

Latissimus dorsi.
This line divides the top of the torso in two in profile.

Posterior superior, iliac spine.

Iliac crest, slanted and fatty.

Anterior superior, iliac spine.

Latissimus dorsi.

The fleshy mass of the external oblique muscle stops at the side of the abdominal muscles.

External oblique muscle.

Teres major.

Latissimus dorsi.
The graphic features on the sides of the torso are almost always apparent on three-quarters-facing and three-quarters-back views, and sometimes even on straight views of the front and back.

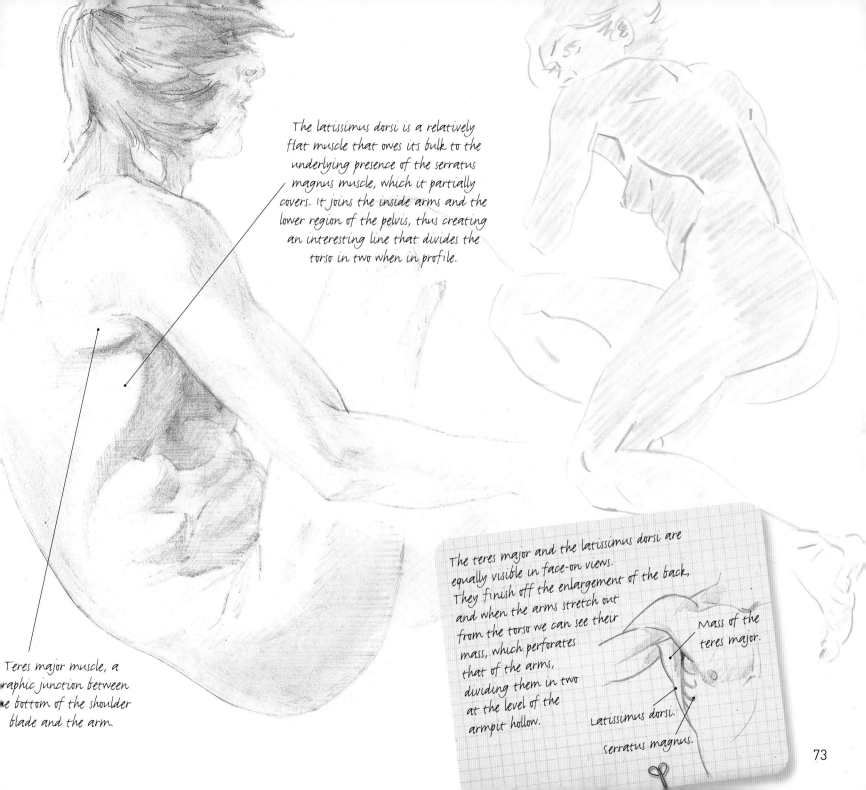

The latissimus dorsi is a relatively flat muscle that owes its bulk to the underlying presence of the serratus magnus muscle, which it partially covers. It joins the inside arms and the lower region of the pelvis, thus creating an interesting line that divides the torso in two when in profile.

Teres major muscle, a graphic junction between the bottom of the shoulder blade and the arm.

The teres major and the latissimus dorsi are equally visible in face-on views. They finish off the enlargement of the back, and when the arms stretch out from the torso we can see their mass, which perforates that of the arms, dividing them in two at the level of the armpit hollow.

Mass of the teres major.

Latissimus dorsi.

serratus magnus.

Serratus magnus

The serratus magnus is a muscle that begins at the bottom of the shoulder blade, like the teres major, but from the other side of the bone. It is, in a way, caught between the shoulder blade and the ribcage. From there, its bundles of fibres move towards the front in a fan shape and attach to the ribs, from the first to the tenth. Only a few of these bundles will be really visible: those located in the middle of the thorax on the side (blue mass, p.42). The beginning of this muscle is hidden by the path of the latissimus dorsi which lets us see its front half. Its endings are fleshy and pointed. The highest are hidden by the pectoral muscle and the lowest by the latissimus dorsi. Most often we can make out six bundles, the most forward being at the level of the base of the pectorals. It is this muscle that begins the enlargement of the back.

Depending on the movements of the arms, the light, or the physical makeup of the person, we do not always see the same things.

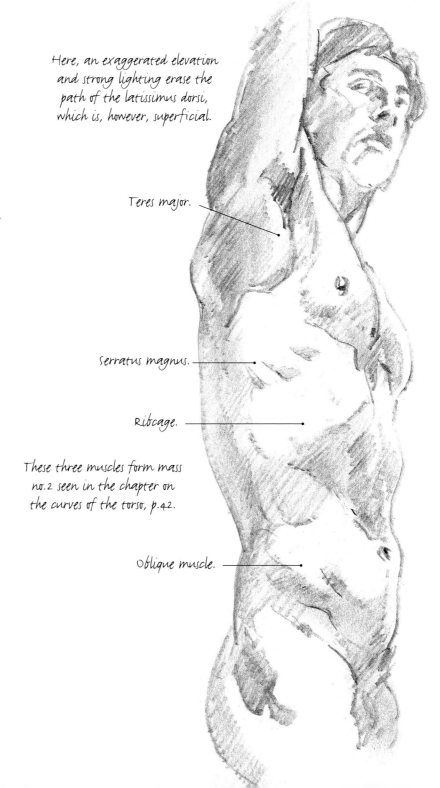

Here, an exaggerated elevation and strong lighting erase the path of the latissimus dorsi, which is, however, superficial.

Teres major.

Serratus magnus.

Ribcage.

These three muscles form mass no.2 seen in the chapter on the curves of the torso, p.42.

Oblique muscle.

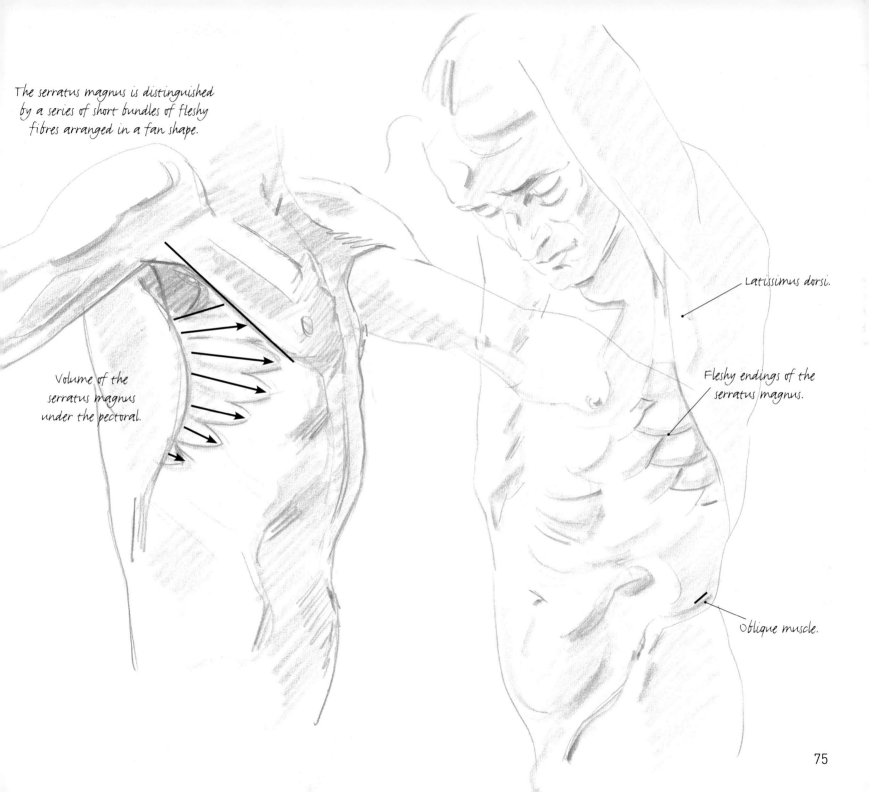

The serratus magnus is distinguished
by a series of short bundles of fleshy
fibres arranged in a fan shape.

Volume of the
serratus magnus
under the pectoral.

Latissimus dorsi.

Fleshy endings of the
serratus magnus.

Oblique muscle.

75

The iliac crest and the oblique muscle

The oblique muscle can be described to be in two parts. The first part is situated at the ribcage level, from which it takes its volume, becoming caught up with the serratus magnus muscle. Its bundles of fibres are directed sideways towards the bottom where they are joined with the abdominal muscles. The second part, placed between the ribcage and the pelvis, is accompanied at the foot by a fatty deposit, giving it a fleshy appearance. It operates as the junction between these two masses on the sides of the torso (blue mass, p.42).

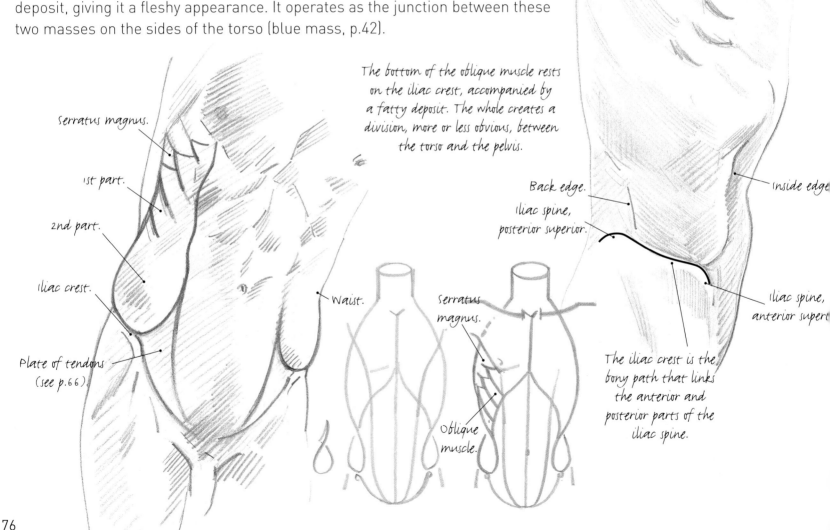

The bottom of the oblique muscle rests on the iliac crest, accompanied by a fatty deposit. The whole creates a division, more or less obvious, between the torso and the pelvis.

Serratus magnus.

1st part.

2nd part.

Iliac crest.

Plate of tendons (see p.66).

Waist.

Serratus magnus.

Oblique muscle.

Back edge.

Iliac spine, posterior superior.

Inside edge

Iliac spine, anterior superior

The iliac crest is the bony path that links the anterior and posterior parts of the iliac spine.

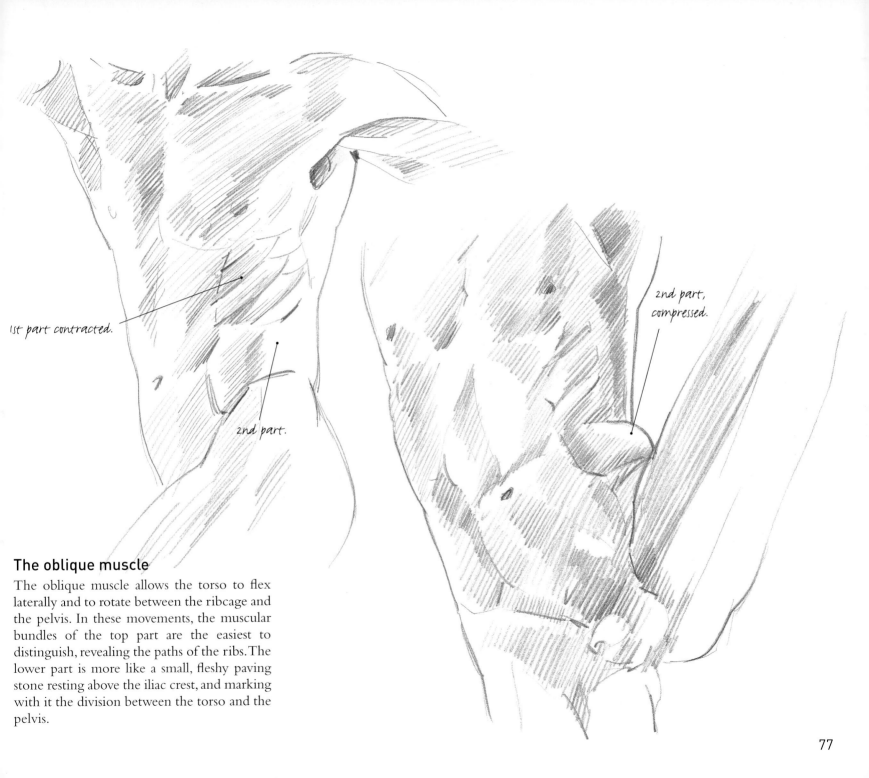

1st part contracted.

2nd part.

2nd part, compressed.

The oblique muscle

The oblique muscle allows the torso to flex laterally and to rotate between the ribcage and the pelvis. In these movements, the muscular bundles of the top part are the easiest to distinguish, revealing the paths of the ribs. The lower part is more like a small, fleshy paving stone resting above the iliac crest, and marking with it the division between the torso and the pelvis.

The lower limbs and the pelvis

Curves and folds when bending

It is still essential to understand and remember how curves are organised.
Especially for the long segments that have two very different profiles.
Here, remember the culminating points of the masses that comprise the
thighs and the legs. Certain movements, such as bending, can change their
composition a little.

Organisation of the main curves and the obliqueness of the shapes

To organise the main curves requires looking
at and deciding on the height of each curve
that makes up the silhouette. On the sides
and behind, the pelvis is surrounded by large
muscle masses. These sketches show the
overlapping of these principal masses.

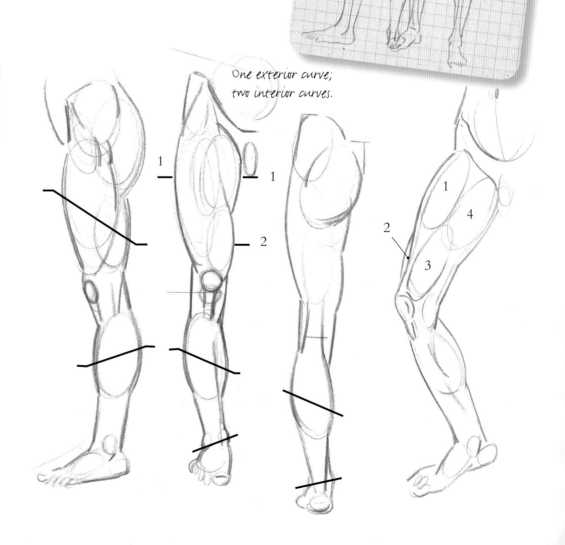

One exterior curve;
two interior curves.

80

A flexing fold

Under the fold of the groin we see a second fold which marks the difference between the region of the pelvis and that of the thigh. This is the flexing fold of the thigh. It descends less than the fold of the groin.

The genitals are often located in its continuation.

The tensor muscle, no.1, crossing the path of the flexing fold of the thigh, is forced to bend, forming with this movement two masses in place of one.

The pelvis

There are three muscles that make up the mass of the pelvis (the part of the trunk that joins the abdomen and the legs):

1 Tensor muscle
2 Gluteus medius
3 Gluteus maximus

A fourth, the sartorius muscle, starts with the tensor of the anterior superior iliac spine and travels to the interior of the thigh where it divides in two on the face and inside profile.

The tensor is suspended from the iliac spine and goes towards the back, where it is placed in front of a small bony knob under the skin belonging to the femur, called the trochanter. The tensor descends slightly below the level of the pubis and is attached to the leg by a large tendon called the fascia lata, clearly visible on the outside of the knee.

The gluteus medius determines the shape of the pelvic region. It is almost a continuation of the oblique muscle, but under the iliac crest. Laterally it occupies the highest and widest part of the pelvis. It is attached to the trochanter at

the level of the pubis (see following chapters).

The gluteus maximus occupies the back of the pelvis. Essentially, it is attached to the sacrum and then runs to the outside behind the trochanter. Its lowest muscle strips are planted in the thigh on the outside, separating the mass of the triceps and biceps (see following pages). It is deeply inserted into the femur.

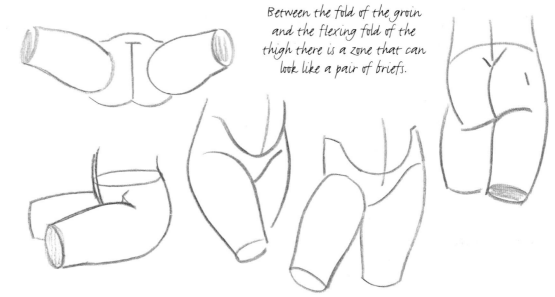

Between the fold of the groin and the flexing fold of the thigh there is a zone that can look like a pair of briefs.

Flexing fold.

The trochanter.

81

The view from the front

Although this chapter deals with the view from the front, many of the elements described will be visible in a wide range of views. I have not dealt with a muscle that is included in the front mass of the thigh, having decided it is too difficult to distinguish. I thus refer to the quadriceps (a muscle of four parts) as the triceps.

When the muscles are relaxed, there are two bulges for one muscle.

slanting mass of the triceps above the kneecap.

1

2

Kneecap.

Fat.

Tibia.

The fatty deposit under the kneecap gives the effect of a double kneecap.

The knees

We find here the slanting mass of the triceps of the thigh above the kneecap.

In front of the knee joint we note two very distinct masses that resemble each other. The first corresponds to the kneecap, the other to a layer of fat situated below. But when the knee is not fatty we can more clearly see a strong tendon under the kneecap, which descends to join the leg. As for the kneecap, this is most easily observed when the leg is slightly bent. When the knee is completely bent, they both tend to disappear; the kneecap seems to be swallowed up in the joint and the tendon and fat are together flattened against the joint. It is this that creates the junction between the thigh and the leg in front. Unlike the elbow, the knee is not pointed when completely bent.

Kneecap.
Bone.

Fatty deposit.

Bony knob of the tibia.

When the muscles are contracted, there is one bulge.

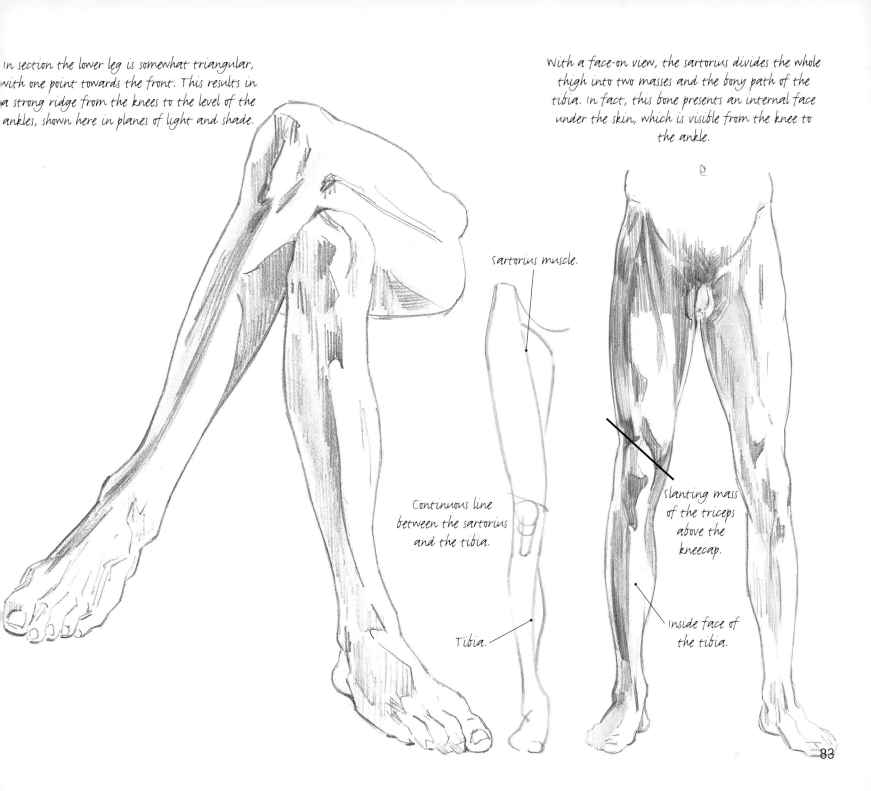

In section the lower leg is somewhat triangular, with one point towards the front. This results in a strong ridge from the knees to the level of the ankles, shown here in planes of light and shade.

With a face-on view, the sartorius divides the whole thigh into two masses and the bony path of the tibia. In fact, this bone presents an internal face under the skin, which is visible from the knee to the ankle.

sartorius muscle.

Continuous line between the sartorius and the tibia.

Tibia.

slanting mass of the triceps above the kneecap.

inside face of the tibia.

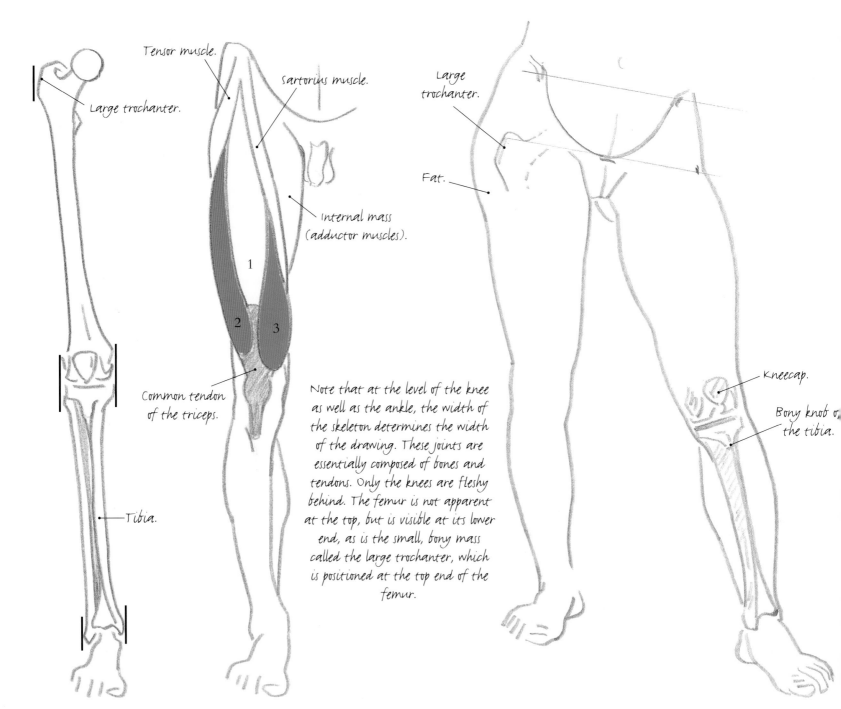

Tensor muscle.

Sartorius muscle.

Large trochanter.

Large trochanter.

Internal mass (adductor muscles).

Fat.

1

2   3

Common tendon of the triceps.

Kneecap.

Bony knob of the tibia.

Tibia.

Note that at the level of the knee as well as the ankle, the width of the skeleton determines the width of the drawing. These joints are essentially composed of bones and tendons. Only the knees are fleshy behind. The femur is not apparent at the top, but is visible at its lower end, as is the small, bony mass called the large trochanter, which is positioned at the top end of the femur.

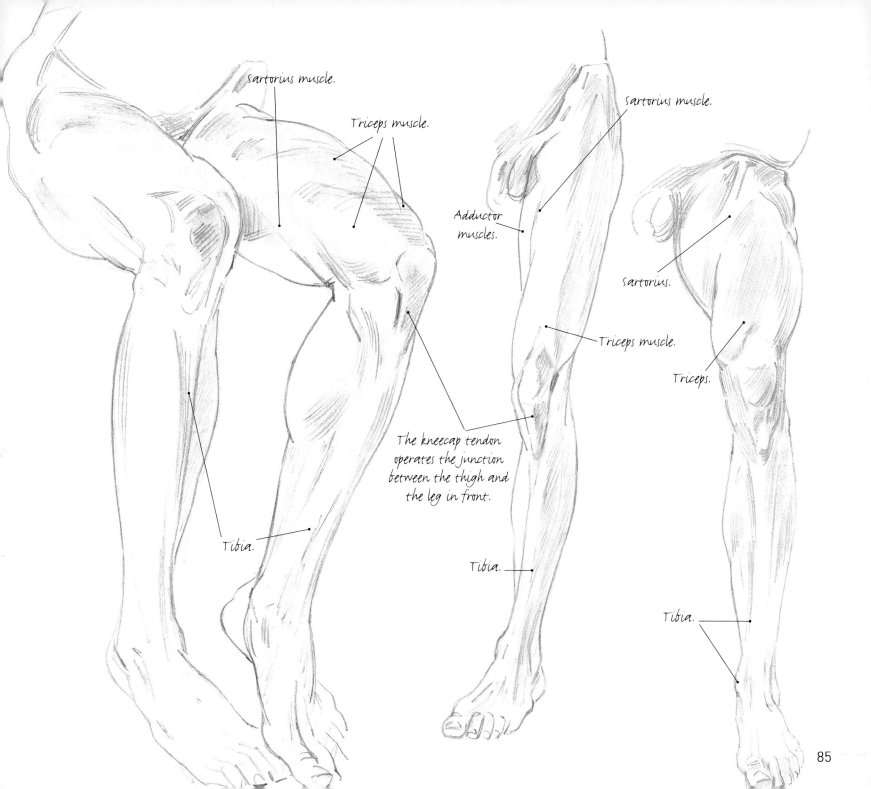

sartorius muscle.

Triceps muscle.

sartorius muscle.

Adductor muscles.

sartorius.

Triceps muscle.

Triceps.

The kneecap tendon operates the junction between the thigh and the leg in front.

Tibia.

Tibia.

Tibia.

Tibia.

85

The view from the back

The back view of the leg comprises, from top to bottom: a fold under the buttocks, two tendons behind the knee and the Achilles tendon. When looking at the back of the leg, the tendons provide the strongest shapes, with the exception of the buttocks.

The knees

In views of the back of the knees, the skeleton disappears behind the muscle mass of the gastrocnemius (calf) which is attached to the bottom of the thigh as it crosses the joint. Below, it is attached to the heel by the strong Achilles tendon.

   The calf muscles accompany a muscle, called the soleus, situated below the calf, which often marks a second mass in the lower half of the leg and on the two sides. These three muscles are arranged behind the leg bones: the tibia and fibula. They make a triceps, united below by the Achilles tendon.

   I call the muscle mass behind the thigh the biceps. This is a simplification of the actual name, but understanding it in this way allows us to show the function of this mass, and the effect of flexing the leg on the thigh. For information, this mass is attached under the gluteus maximus, at the lower end of the pelvis. It also allows the rotation of the leg in relation to the thigh when flexed and helps to lift the body, pulling on the pelvis when the legs are stretched.

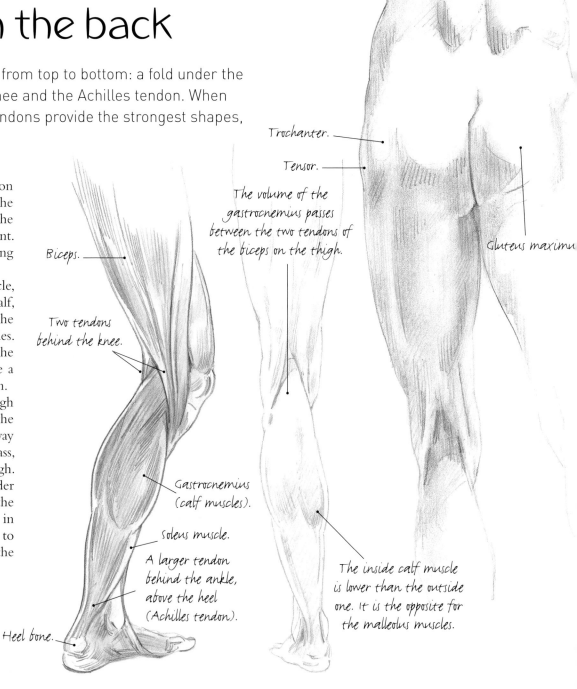

Trochanter.

Tensor.

The volume of the gastrocnemius passes between the two tendons of the biceps on the thigh.

Gluteus maximu

Biceps.

Two tendons behind the knee.

Gastrocnemius (calf muscles).

Soleus muscle.

A larger tendon behind the ankle, above the heel (Achilles tendon).

Heel bone.

The inside calf muscle is lower than the outside one. It is the opposite for the malleolus muscles.

A graphic simplification

There are two important skills necessary to achieve a realistic drawing. The first is the ability to analyse the silhouette and reproduce it; the second is to place the graphic elements inside the outline. However, although a perfectly outlined silhouette does not go well with a badly placed navel or kneecap (upsetting the 'reading' of the drawing), well-positioned graphic elements enhance a silhouette even when it is only sketchy or partially drawn. In other words, the graphic elements inside a shape are more expressive than the silhouette itself. You can thus plan not to finish the contours of your drawing, whether they are in line or in grey tones.

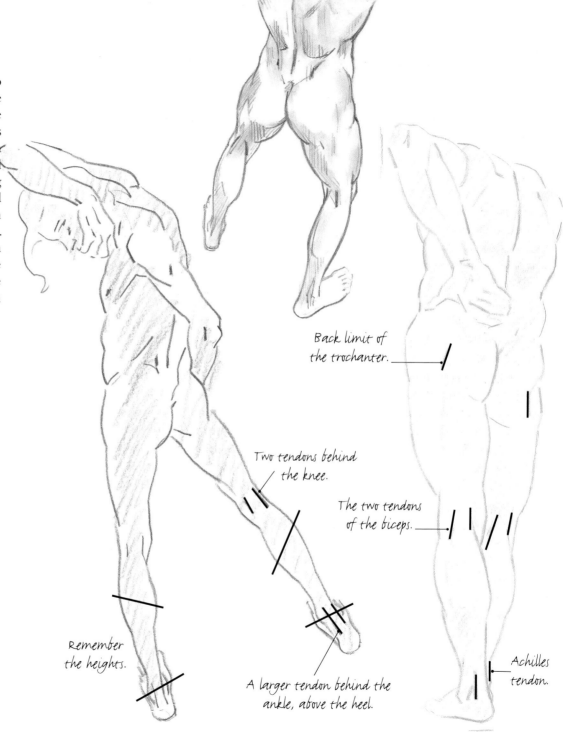

Back limit of the trochanter.

Two tendons behind the knee.

The two tendons of the biceps.

Remember the heights.

A larger tendon behind the ankle, above the heel.

Achilles tendon.

87

The sartorius and the tibia: another long line

The silhouette of the outside profile is indeed identical to that of the inside profile. And here also we will find elements belonging to the view from the front and from the back.

The inside profile

The sartorius is the longest muscle in the human body. It starts from the iliac spine mentioned earlier and finishes at the top of the lower leg, after having enveloped the internal face of the knee as it twists round.

The lower part of this muscle joins the tibia, a pillar of bone that finishes above the foot, creating the inside malleolus (ankle bone).

The path of the sartorius and tibia leaves from the pelvis and crosses the whole height of the lower limb, dividing in two just at the foot. It resembles a wide ribbon, slightly twisted.

At thigh level, we find the continuous line already shown on the front view, created by the sartorius and the tibia, in front of which is the inside bundle of the triceps of the thigh in contact with the kneecap.

For the lower leg, the most remarkable elements are formed by the fleshy inside calf, as well as the malleolus and the Achilles tendon.

On the front and outside leg, there is a fleshy muscle (inside leg muscle) whose tendon crosses the ankle joint in front to attach to the middle of the foot at the side of the instep. This tendon, which we will see in the chapter on the foot, is an important element in the transition between leg and foot. It is the curve of the inside leg muscle that defines the profile of the lower leg. Thus, it slightly overflows the bony path of the tibia.

sartorius.

Kneecap and under-tendon.

Inside gastrocnemius.

soleus.

Tibia.

Inside leg muscle.

Tibia.

Inside leg muscle.

Inside malleolus (ankle bone), higher and more square than the outside malleolus.

Tendon of the inside leg muscle.

We find here one of the most interesting paths of the human body, already powerful in the frontal view.

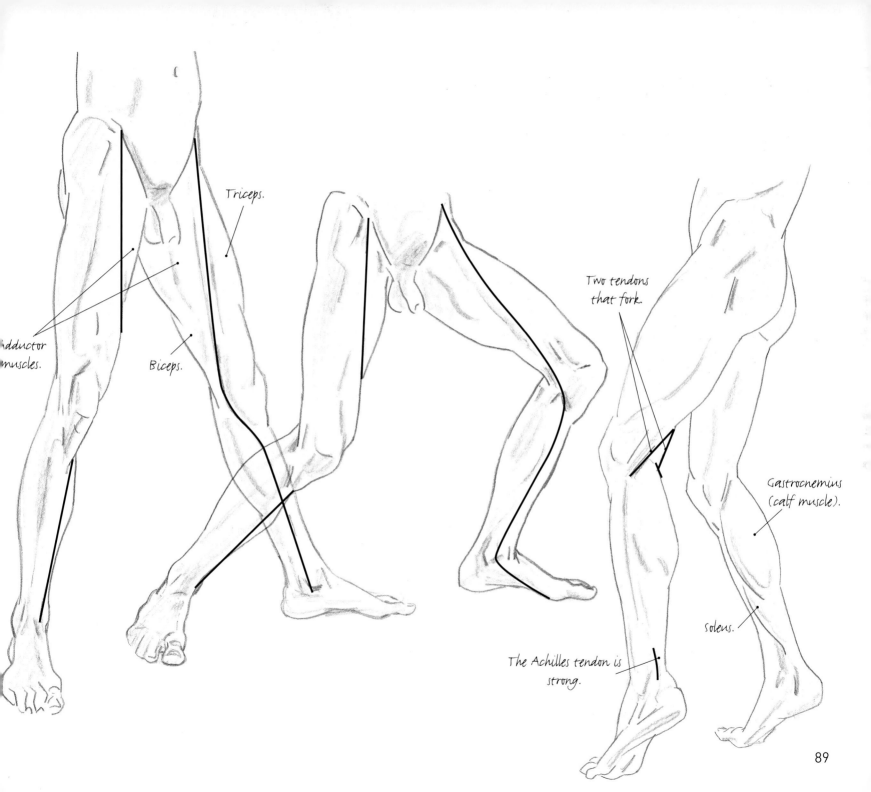

Triceps.

Biceps.

adductor
muscles.

Two tendons
that fork.

Gastrocnemius
(calf muscle).

soleus.

The Achilles tendon is
strong.

89

Trochanter and the vastus externus

The trochanter is the end of the collar of the femur and the only point where the thigh bone emerges near the pelvis. It marks the beginning of the thigh. The trochanters impinge on the pelvis, which makes the distance that separates them the largest inter-axis after that of the shoulders. Suspended on this little knob of bone, the external muscular bundle of the triceps of the thigh crosses the segment to join the kneecap with its tendon.

A third cord at knee level

The gigantic tendon of the tensor crosses the whole length of the thigh to finish at the outside top of the lower leg. From it runs a supplementary tendon which goes through the knee joint.

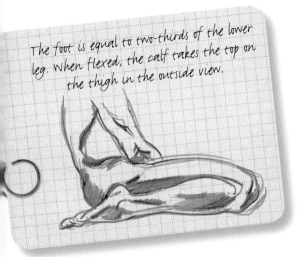

The foot is equal to two-thirds of the lower leg. When flexed, the calf takes the top on the thigh in the outside view.

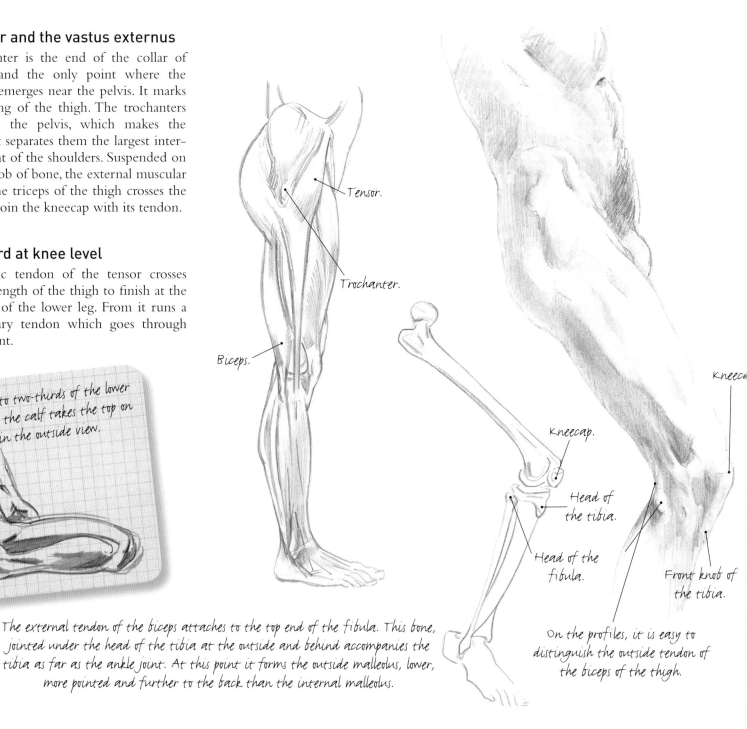

Tensor.

Trochanter.

Biceps.

Kneecap.

Head of the tibia.

Head of the fibula.

Kneec[ap]

Front knob of the tibia.

The external tendon of the biceps attaches to the top end of the fibula. This bone, jointed under the head of the tibia at the outside and behind accompanies the tibia as far as the ankle joint. At this point it forms the outside malleolus, lower, more pointed and further to the back than the internal malleolus.

On the profiles, it is easy to distinguish the outside tendon of the biceps of the thigh.

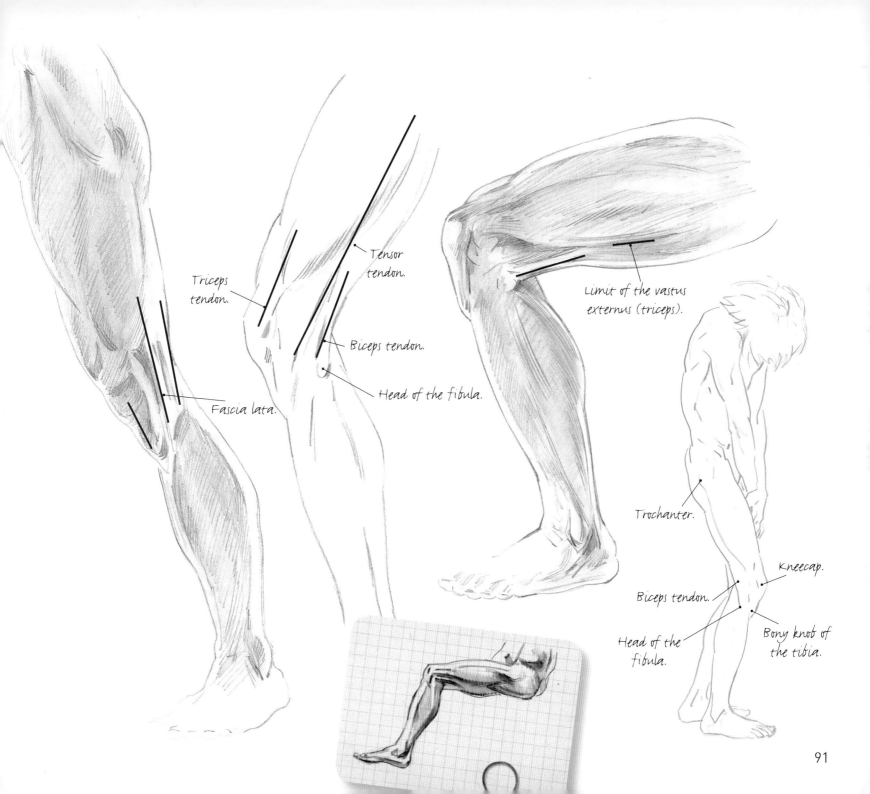

Triceps
tendon.

Tensor
tendon.

Biceps tendon.

Head of the fibula.

Fascia lata.

Limit of the vastus
externus (triceps).

Trochanter.

Kneecap.

Biceps tendon.

Head of the
fibula.

Bony knob of
the tibia.

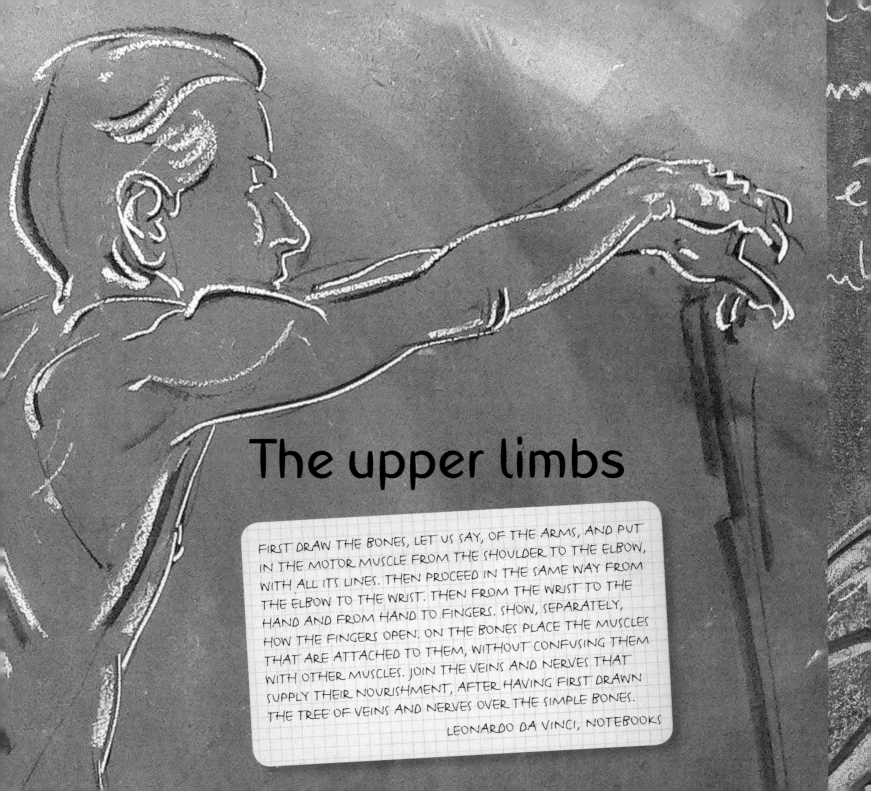

The upper limbs

FIRST DRAW THE BONES, LET US SAY, OF THE ARMS, AND PUT IN THE MOTOR MUSCLE FROM THE SHOULDER TO THE ELBOW, WITH ALL ITS LINES. THEN PROCEED IN THE SAME WAY FROM THE ELBOW TO THE WRIST. THEN FROM THE WRIST TO THE HAND AND FROM HAND TO FINGERS. SHOW, SEPARATELY, HOW THE FINGERS OPEN. ON THE BONES PLACE THE MUSCLES THAT ARE ATTACHED TO THEM, WITHOUT CONFUSING THEM WITH OTHER MUSCLES. JOIN THE VEINS AND NERVES THAT SUPPLY THEIR NOURISHMENT, AFTER HAVING FIRST DRAWN THE TREE OF VEINS AND NERVES OVER THE SIMPLE BONES.

LEONARDO DA VINCI, NOTEBOOKS

The curves

In this chapter I have decided not to show the skeleton of the arms and the forearms whose mechanism is interesting but less visible than it is at the knee.

Contrasting the profiles

The inside profile of an arm or a thigh is very different from the outside profile. These contrasts allow us to avoid symmetry and thus a 'sausage' effect, which looks a little naïve.

Look at each curve closely before drawing it, and consider where it finishes in relation to the curve opposite.

On the upper arm we find a biceps and a triceps muscle – as for the forearm – and, squeezed between the two, a muscle called the

brachialis that goes with the biceps.

On the face-on view, the triceps overflows on top of the two sides of the arm.

At the crook of the elbow, the mass of the biceps stops sideways, descending lower to the inside. For the forearm, we can consider that the height of masses 1 and 2 will be in complementary positions. It is the volume of mass 3 that creates asymmetry in the profiles.

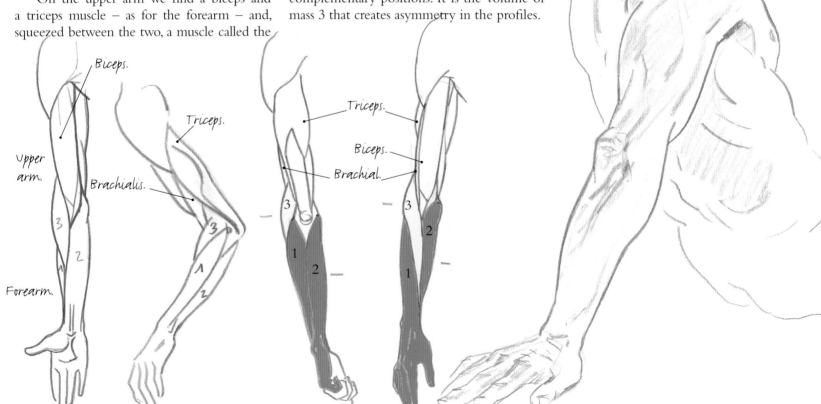

Biceps.

Triceps.

Upper
arm.

Brachialis.

Triceps.

Biceps.

Brachial.

Forearm.

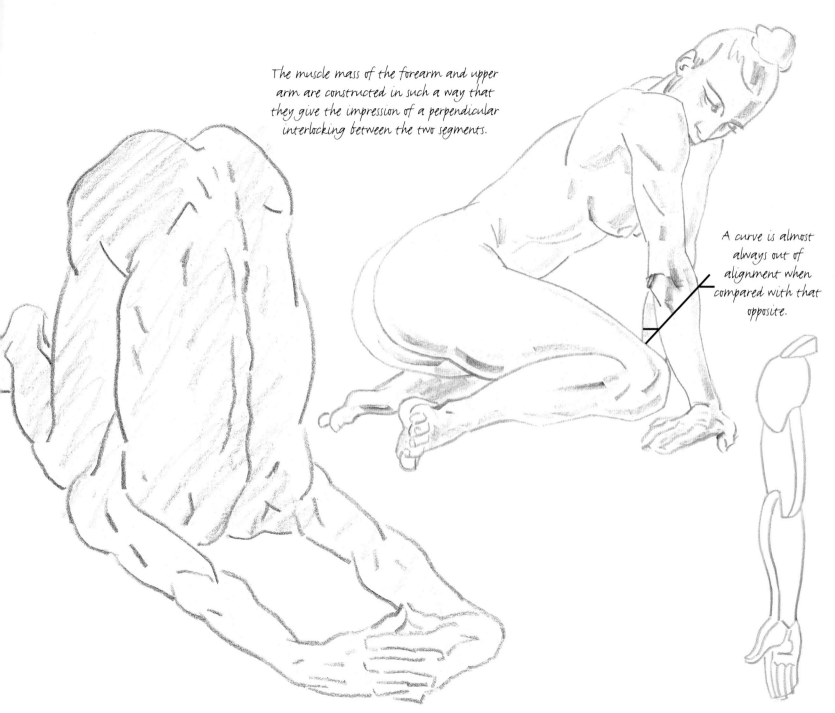

The muscle mass of the forearm and upper arm are constructed in such a way that they give the impression of a perpendicular interlocking between the two segments.

A curve is almost always out of alignment when compared with that opposite.

The upper limb face-on

Seen face-on, the arm, forearm and hand do not appear bony. Nevertheless, their shapes are partly determined by the muscles and tendons. Obviously, the size of the musculature is the main factor when deciding how much emphasis should be given to these graphic shapes.

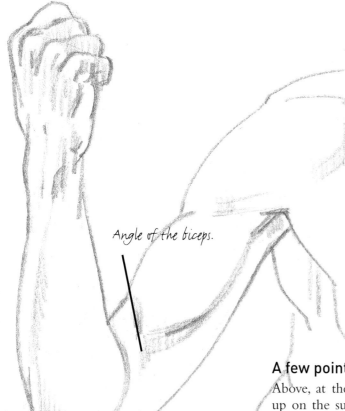

Angle of the biceps.

Face on, or from the back with arms held out, the forearm is not on the axis of the upper arm and turns towards the outside. This angle is often wider in women. When the hand turns inwards, we find an alignment between the two sections: it brings with it the muscular mass previously located on the outside.

A few points of reference

Above, at the level of the shoulder, moving up on the summit of the arm bone, we can identify two muscle bunches in the movement of raising the arm. Below, on the mass of the arm, we can make out the passage of the pectoral muscle, seen before (see p.56).

Then, we have to approach the crook of the elbow to find clear graphic information.

At this spot there is a slight hollow which marks a little shady zone created by the surrounding muscle masses. The slant at the base of the biceps will be equally visible. It descends lower towards the inside.

Before arriving at the palm of the hand, two tendons animate the most fleshy region of the wrist.

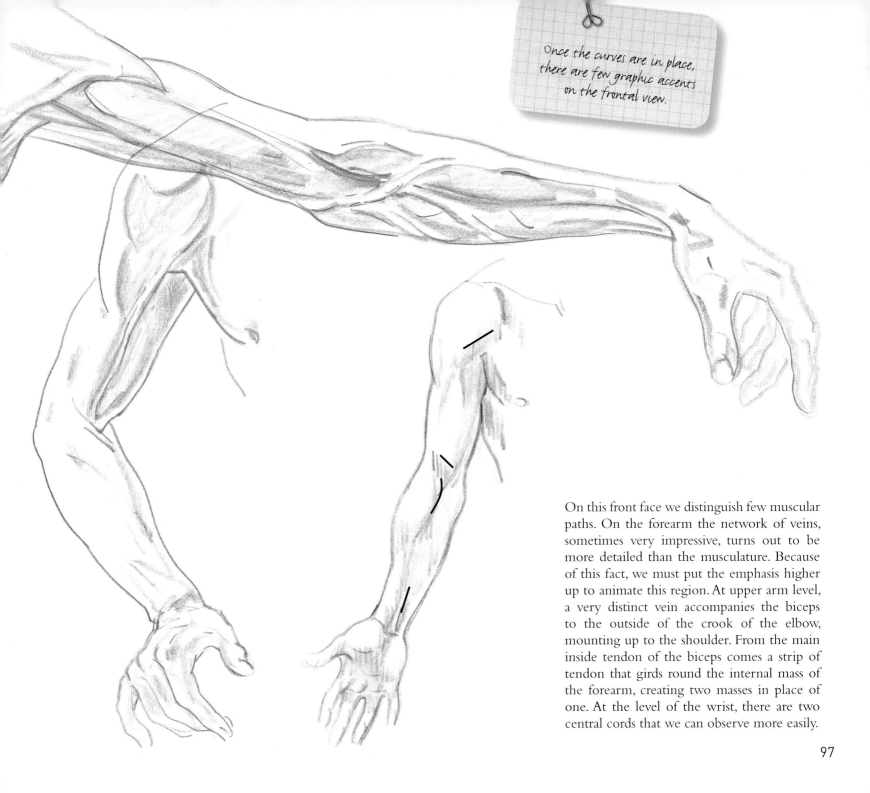

Once the curves are in place, there are few graphic accents on the frontal view.

On this front face we distinguish few muscular paths. On the forearm the network of veins, sometimes very impressive, turns out to be more detailed than the musculature. Because of this fact, we must put the emphasis higher up to animate this region. At upper arm level, a very distinct vein accompanies the biceps to the outside of the crook of the elbow, mounting up to the shoulder. From the main inside tendon of the biceps comes a strip of tendon that girds round the internal mass of the forearm, creating two masses in place of one. At the level of the wrist, there are two central cords that we can observe more easily.

The upper limb from the back

In contrast with the frontal view, in the back view, the arm, forearm and hand have several bony landmarks, starting with the elbow.

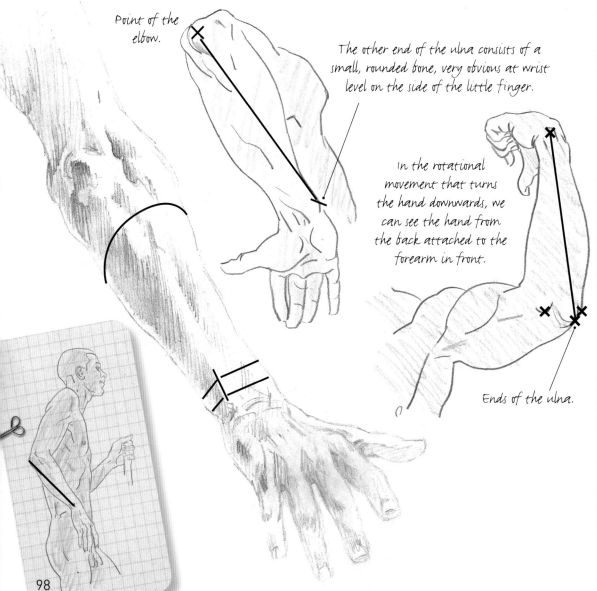

Point of the elbow.

The other end of the ulna consists of a small, rounded bone, very obvious at wrist level on the side of the little finger.

In the rotational movement that turns the hand downwards, we can see the hand from the back attached to the forearm in front.

Ends of the ulna.

The shoulder

From the back, the shoulder is not obvious, but shows up in strong lifting movements of the arm, where a line joins the shoulder blade and the outside arm.

The mass of the triceps, on the other hand, has large graphic value when it is in contraction (see opposite, p.99).

The elbow

This has three easily-seen bony points, one of which moves when the forearm is bent. These three points are aligned when the forearm is outstretched. The central point is lowered during bending movements, thus forming a triangle with the other two.

Note that there are clear muscular paths that run from an outside point to the back of the hand.

A careful placing of these three points gives a good 'reading' of the many positions of the upper limb. At rest, the forearms are lightly flexed and the elbows are slightly pointed outwards.

The wrist

At the level of the wrist, above the back of the hand, and on the side of the little finger, we can observe a small round mass corresponding to the end of one of the two bones of the forearm: the ulna.

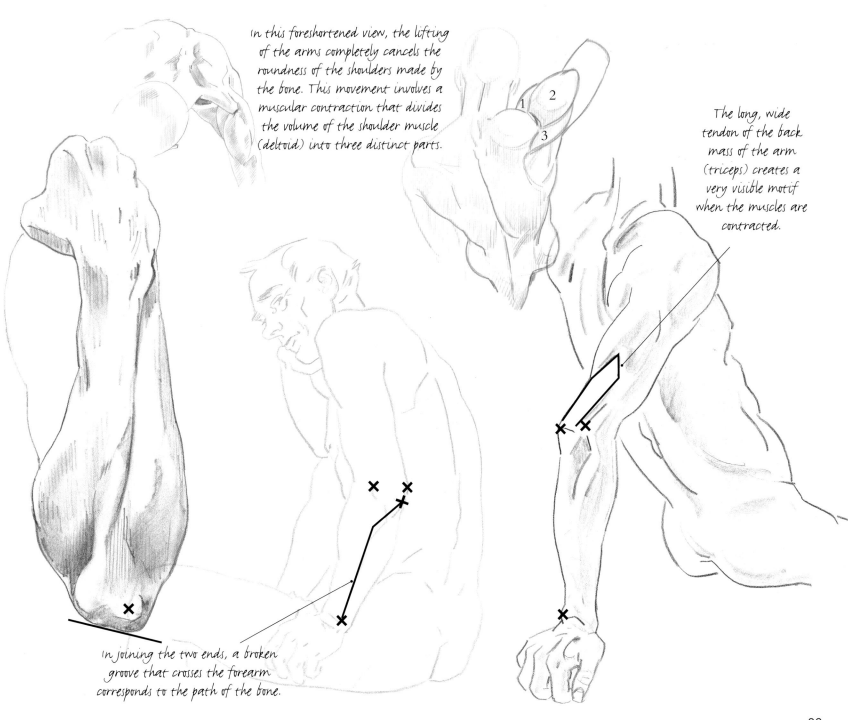

In this foreshortened view, the lifting of the arms completely cancels the roundness of the shoulders made by the bone. This movement involves a muscular contraction that divides the volume of the shoulder muscle (deltoid) into three distinct parts.

1
2
3

The long, wide tendon of the back mass of the arm (triceps) creates a very visible motif when the muscles are contracted.

In joining the two ends, a broken groove that crosses the forearm corresponds to the path of the bone.

The upper limb in profile

As with the thigh, we revisit the elements already seen in other views. Here, it is the biceps that plays the main part.

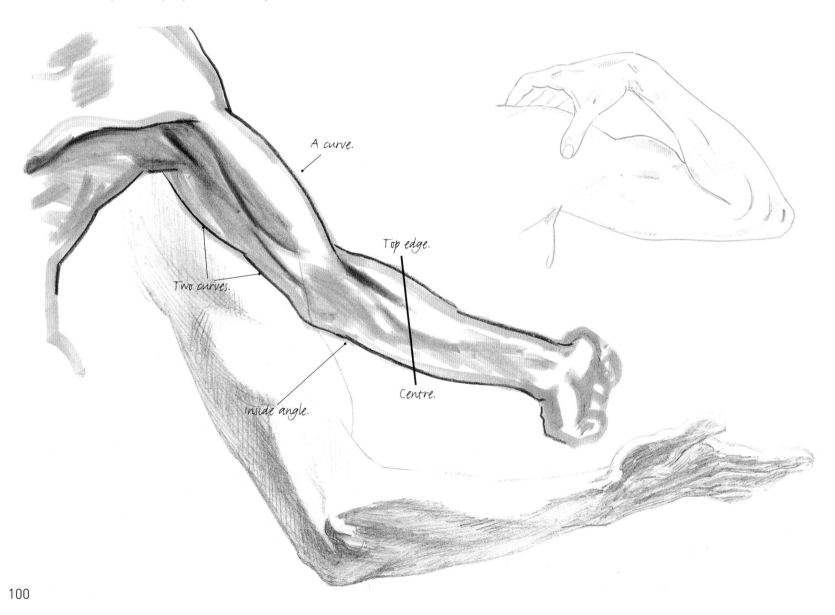

A curve.

Two curves.

Top edge.

Centre.

inside angle.

This drawing shows an arm in profile, in an anatomical position, that is to say, stretched down and hand open. It is not a natural position.

One of the most important elements in a profile is that the shoulder does not divide the volume of the arm into two equal parts. It is inserted just in front of the biceps, thus clearly towards the front.

End of the shoulder mass.

Top of the triceps.

Top of the triceps lower.

Here the arm is still too stretched out, but the positions of the elbow and hand are more natural (elbow slightly towards the outside and back of the hand, turned towards the front).

The asymmetry of the profiles of the forearm are more obvious in movements of pronation (rotation of the hand towards the inside).

The point of the elbow lowers when the forearm is bent, involving the triceps and making the top move down. The biceps is very round when flexed but flat when extended.

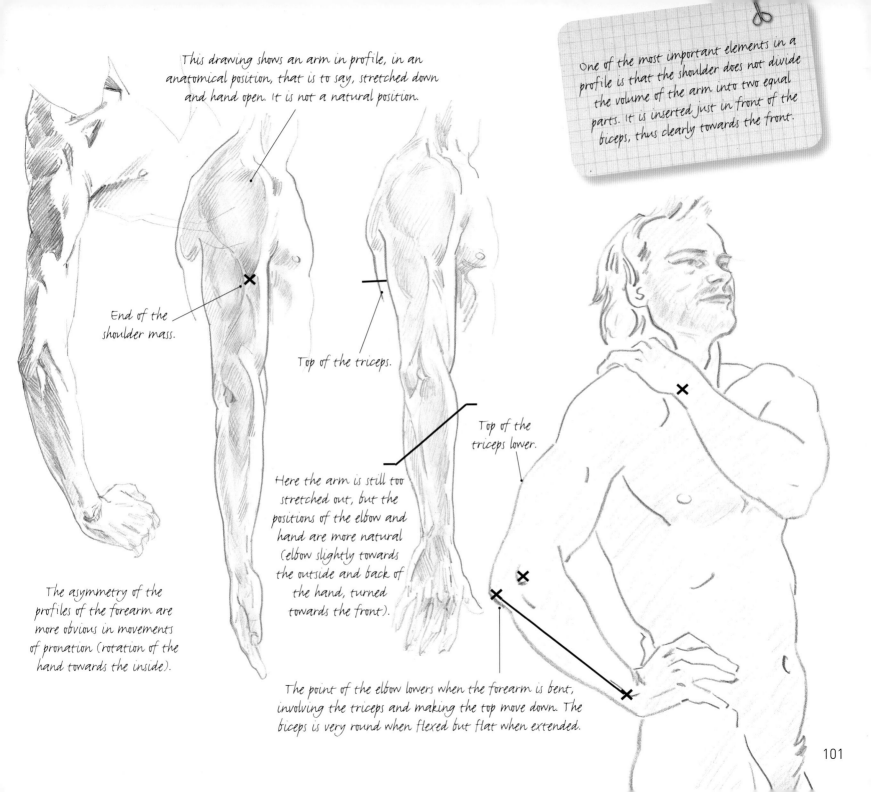

101

Comparing elbows and knees

In this chapter I will simply show the joints of the elbows and knees by comparing them.

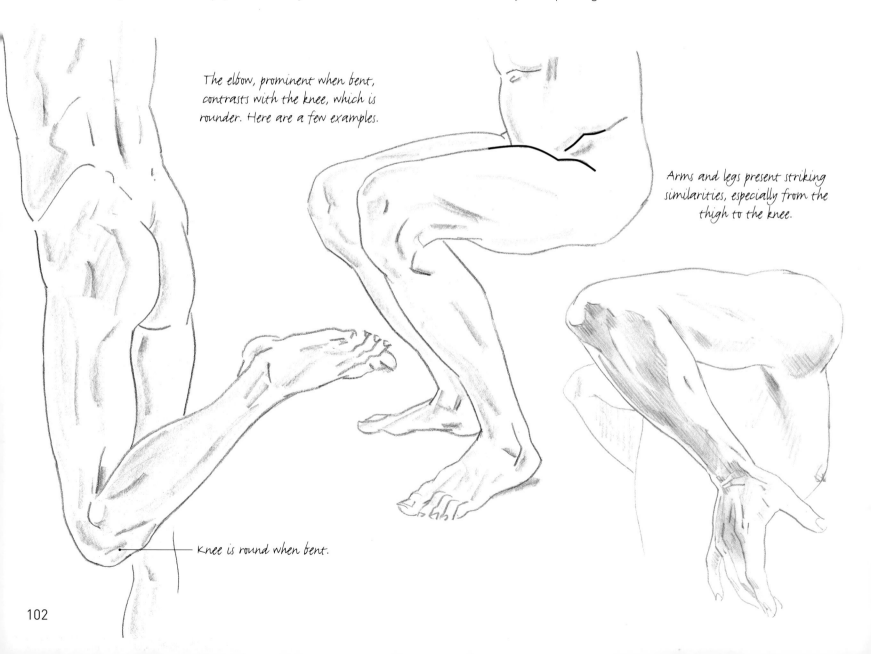

The elbow, prominent when bent, contrasts with the knee, which is rounder. Here are a few examples.

Arms and legs present striking similarities, especially from the thigh to the knee.

Knee is round when bent.

Contrast of elbow and knee. When bent, the elbow always has a more pointed shape than the knee.

Elbow pointed when bent.

Summary

These drawings were made with a large felt-tip during a sketching session, which imposed an exercise in style. I have tried to put in highlights corresponding to the various elements explained in the previous chapters.

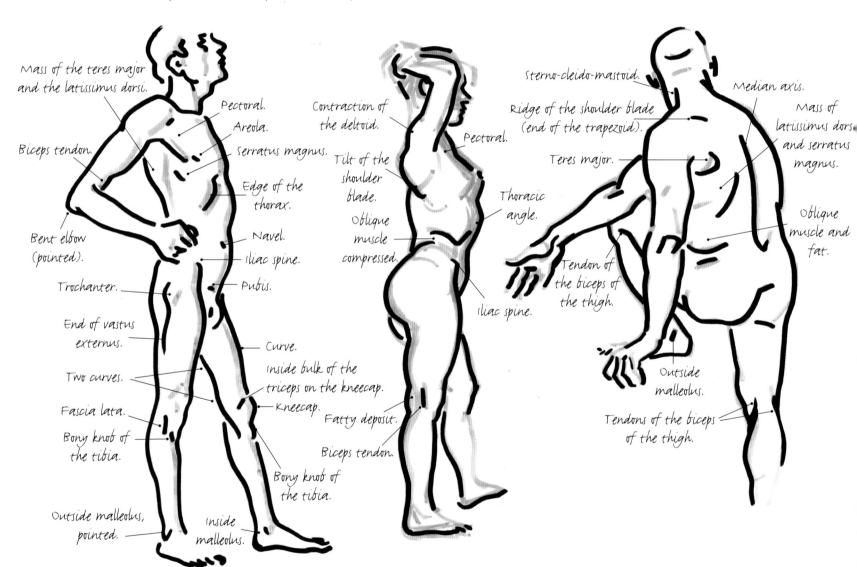

Mass of the teres major and the latissimus dorsi.

Pectoral.

Areola.

Biceps tendon.

Serratus magnus.

Edge of the thorax.

Bent elbow (pointed).

Navel.

Iliac spine.

Trochanter.

Pubis.

End of vastus externus.

Curve.

Inside bulk of the triceps on the kneecap.

Two curves.

Kneecap.

Fascia lata.

Bony knob of the tibia.

Outside malleolus, pointed.

Inside malleolus.

Bony knob of the tibia.

Contraction of the deltoid.

Pectoral.

Tilt of the shoulder blade.

Oblique muscle compressed.

Iliac spine.

Fatty deposit.

Biceps tendon.

Sterno-cleido-mastoid.

Ridge of the shoulder blade (end of the trapezoid).

Teres major.

Thoracic angle.

Tendon of the biceps of the thigh.

Median axis.

Mass of latissimus dorsi and serratus magnus.

Oblique muscle and fat.

Outside malleolus.

Tendons of the biceps of the thigh.

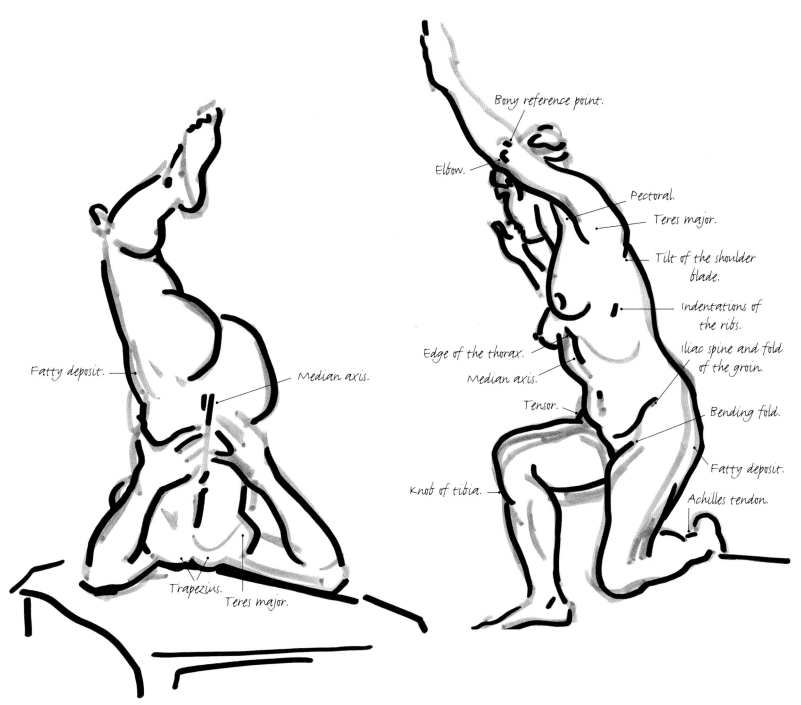

Fatty deposit.

Median axis.

Trapezius.

Teres major.

Bony reference point.

Elbow.

Pectoral.

Teres major.

Tilt of the shoulder blade.

Indentations of the ribs.

Edge of the thorax.

Iliac spine and fold of the groin.

Median axis.

Tensor.

Bending fold.

Knob of tibia.

Fatty deposit.

Achilles tendon.

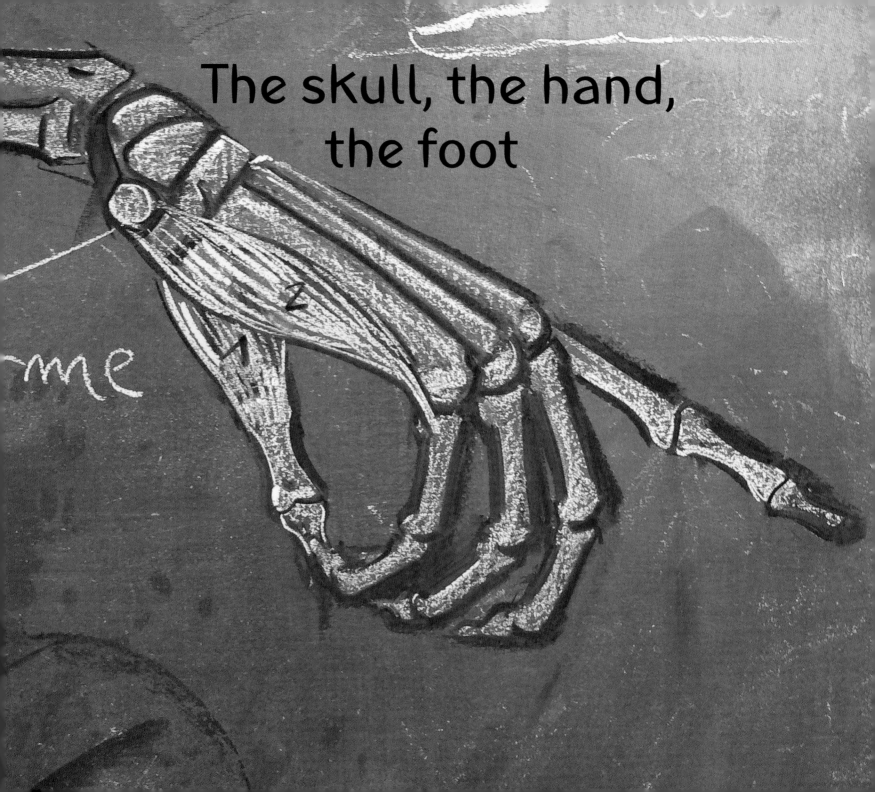

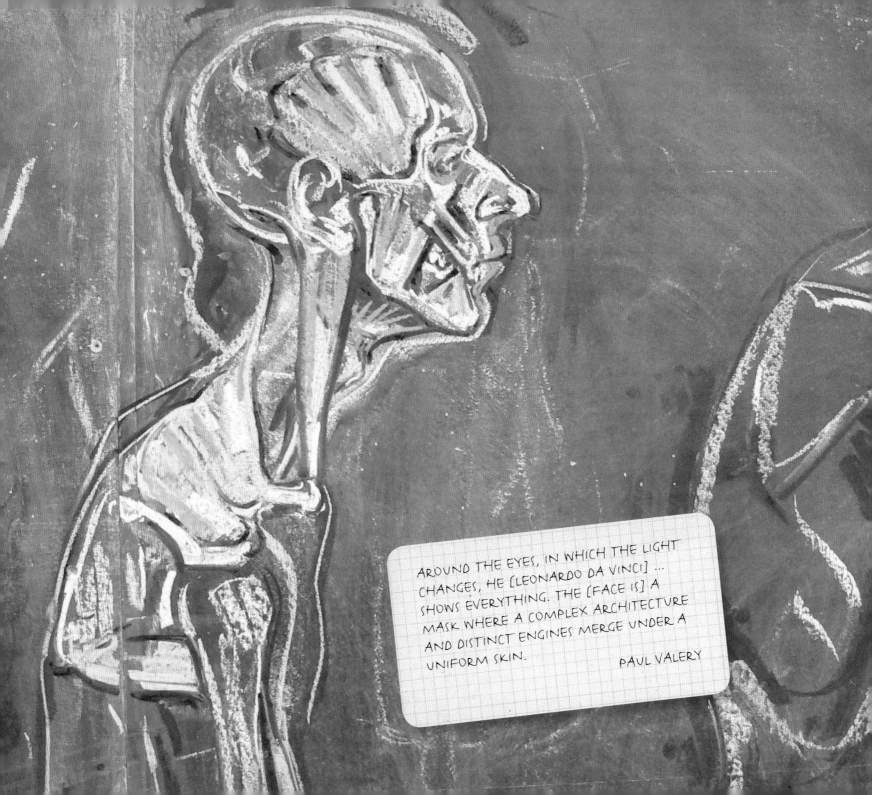

AROUND THE EYES, IN WHICH THE LIGHT
CHANGES, HE [LEONARDO DA VINCI] ...
SHOWS EVERYTHING. THE [FACE IS] A
MASK WHERE A COMPLEX ARCHITECTURE
AND DISTINCT ENGINES MERGE UNDER A
UNIFORM SKIN.

PAUL VALERY

The skull

We can consider the skull to be composed of three parts: the cranium, the face and the lower jaw, the only movable part. If we ignore the lower region, entirely hidden by the neck, we can say that only the lips hide the structure of the skull.

The most important element is the mask, consisting of the eye sockets, cheekbones and an extended arch that gives the face its shape. The mask determines the facial traits.

To put in place the different elements that make up the head, especially the face, I advise positioning the gaze (use two black dots), the ears and the chin in relation to the nearest shoulder. Then draw the eyebrows, the nose and the mouth. For the characteristics of the face we can choose to emphasize the cheekbones, the jawline or the folds that create the expression – the result of muscular contractions.

The eyes are always in the middle of the entire volume of the head. Thus, in perspective views, we can draw a curve corresponding to the path they are going to follow (see the captions on the drawings).

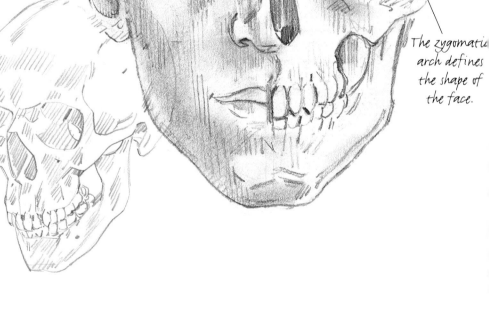

The zygomatic arch defines the shape of the face.

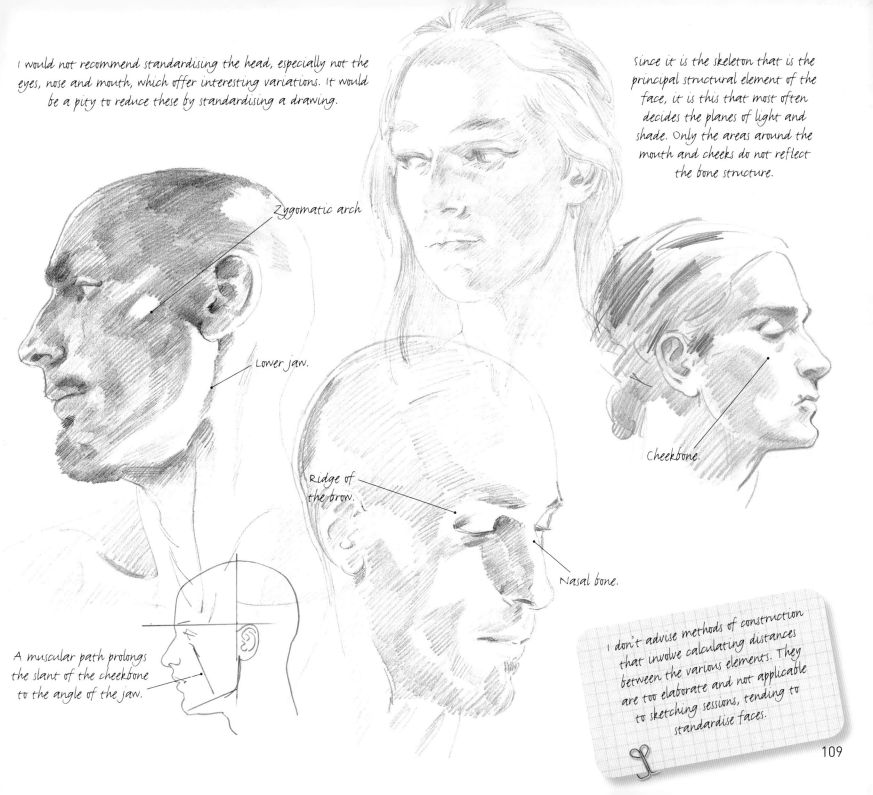

I would not recommend standardising the head, especially not the eyes, nose and mouth, which offer interesting variations. It would be a pity to reduce these by standardising a drawing.

Since it is the skeleton that is the principal structural element of the face, it is this that most often decides the planes of light and shade. Only the areas around the mouth and cheeks do not reflect the bone structure.

Zygomatic arch

Lower jaw.

Ridge of the brow.

Nasal bone.

Cheekbone.

A muscular path prolongs the slant of the cheekbone to the angle of the jaw.

I don't advise methods of construction that involve calculating distances between the various elements. They are too elaborate and not applicable to sketching sessions, tending to standardise faces.

109

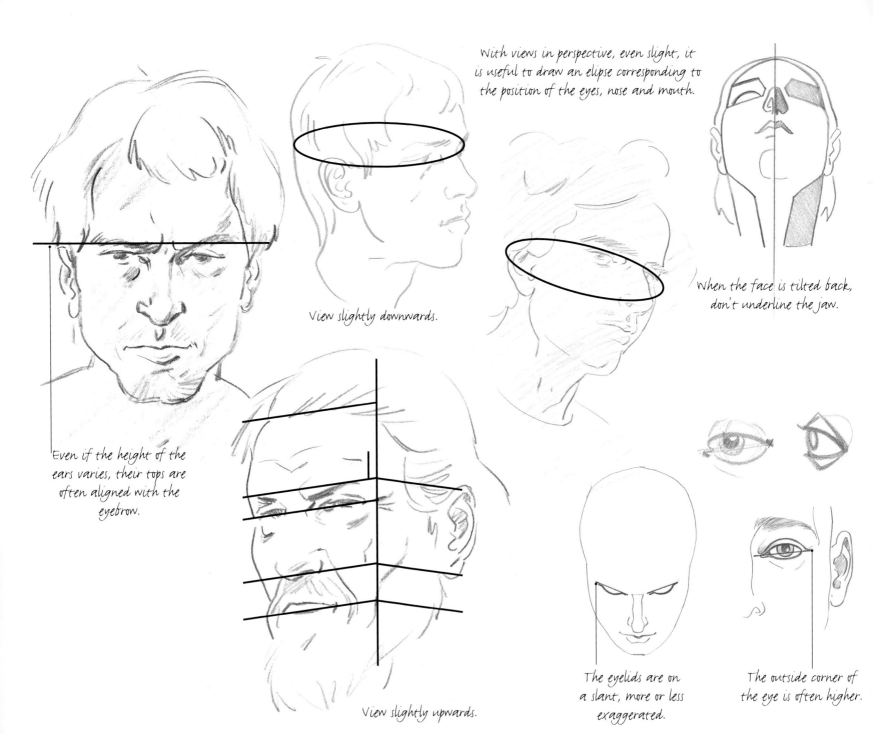

With views in perspective, even slight, it is useful to draw an elipse corresponding to the position of the eyes, nose and mouth.

View slightly downwards.

When the face is tilted back, don't underline the jaw.

Even if the height of the ears varies, their tops are often aligned with the eyebrow.

View slightly upwards.

The eyelids are on a slant, more or less exaggerated.

The outside corner of the eye is often higher.

A few sketches

The shape of the hair, when the style is simple, reinforces the mass of the skull.

Between the eyes there is space for a third.

Sometimes the shape is very difficult to determine...

The ear

Like all the small elements of the body, the difficulty is in their suggestion. In the overall scheme it is important not to give too much detail, while still making them comprehensible.

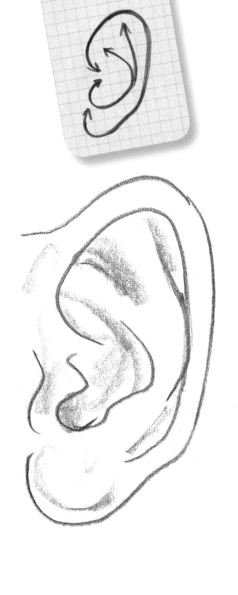

Placing the ear

The height of the ear is variable, and is generally thought to be higher in women.

Finding the correct position helps when drawing a view of a head in perspective.

The ear is situated at the side, on the back half of the head. The wedge-shaped cartilage that attaches the ears to the skull orientates the whole auricle towards the front. Its shape can be described as a rimmed outline rather than an oval. Inside is a second bumpy shape, curving towards the back and forked towards the top. This arrangement creates the hollows, and so the areas of shadow.

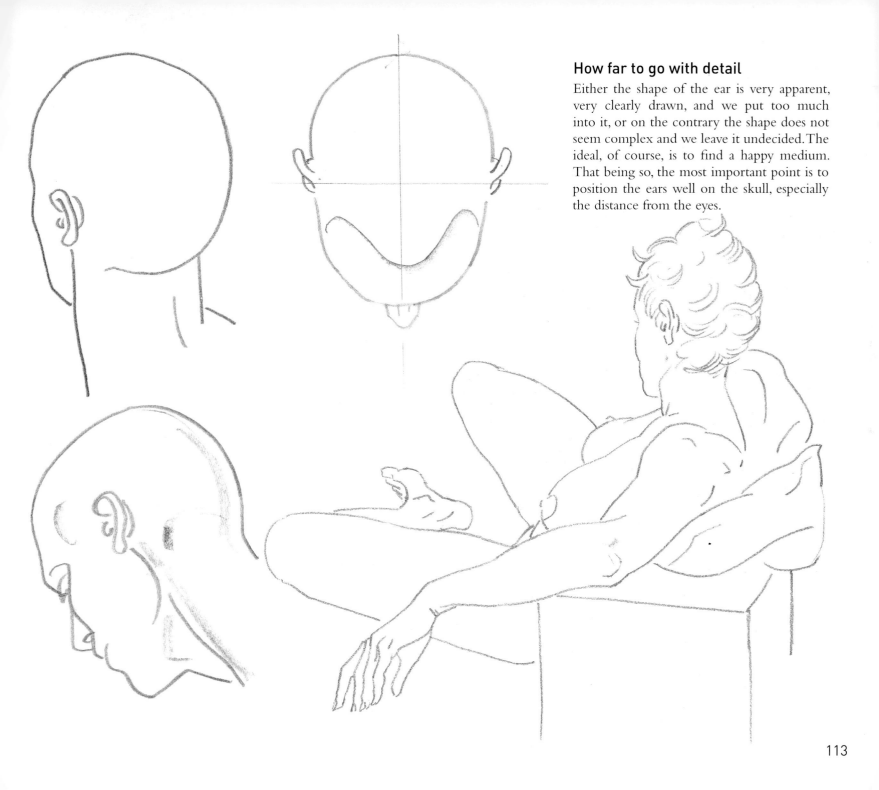

How far to go with detail

Either the shape of the ear is very apparent, very clearly drawn, and we put too much into it, or on the contrary the shape does not seem complex and we leave it undecided. The ideal, of course, is to find a happy medium. That being so, the most important point is to position the ears well on the skull, especially the distance from the eyes.

The wrist and the hand

The extremities are very difficult to draw, especially the hands, which consist of so many bony points. However, there are some small points to know that can help you.

Bending and extending

The wrist can be badly distorted, complicating the drawing of extreme movements of bending or extending the hand. The most common mistake is to bend the wrist at a right angle, thus creating a stiffness. Looking more closely, we see a small intermediate line between the forearm and the arm in one or another of these two movements. Extending movements are always accompanied by folds of skin. The back of the hand, like that of the foot, is essentially bones and tendons.

The index finger and little finger often have a slight curve inwards. In repose, without any specific movement, the thumb is below the level of the other fingers. The middle finger is always the longest and the little finger the shortest. On the other hand the index finger and the ring finger can have the same size or dispute the second place, after the middle finger.

We find two tendons at the wrist going towards the palm of the hand.

The thumb is missing a joint but keeps three mobile segments.

On the back of the hand, hand extended, a fan of four cylindrical tendons show clearly under the skin. Three are most often seen. They are in line with the axis of the fingers, except for the thumb.

The index finger.

The middle finger.

The ring finger.

The little finger.

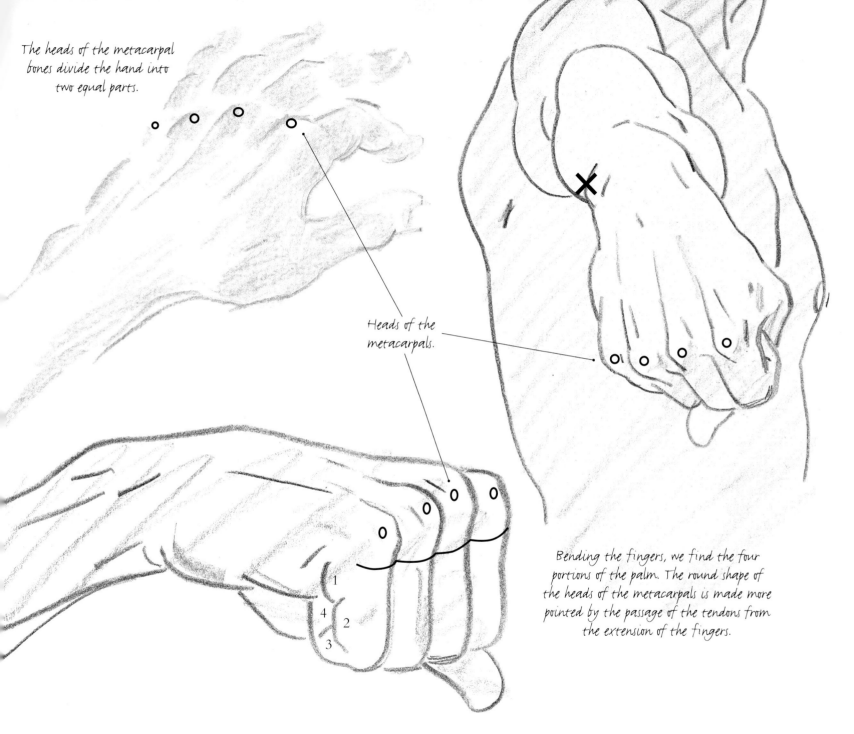

The heads of the metacarpal bones divide the hand into two equal parts.

Heads of the metacarpals.

Bending the fingers, we find the four portions of the palm. The round shape of the heads of the metacarpals is made more pointed by the passage of the tendons from the extension of the fingers.

115

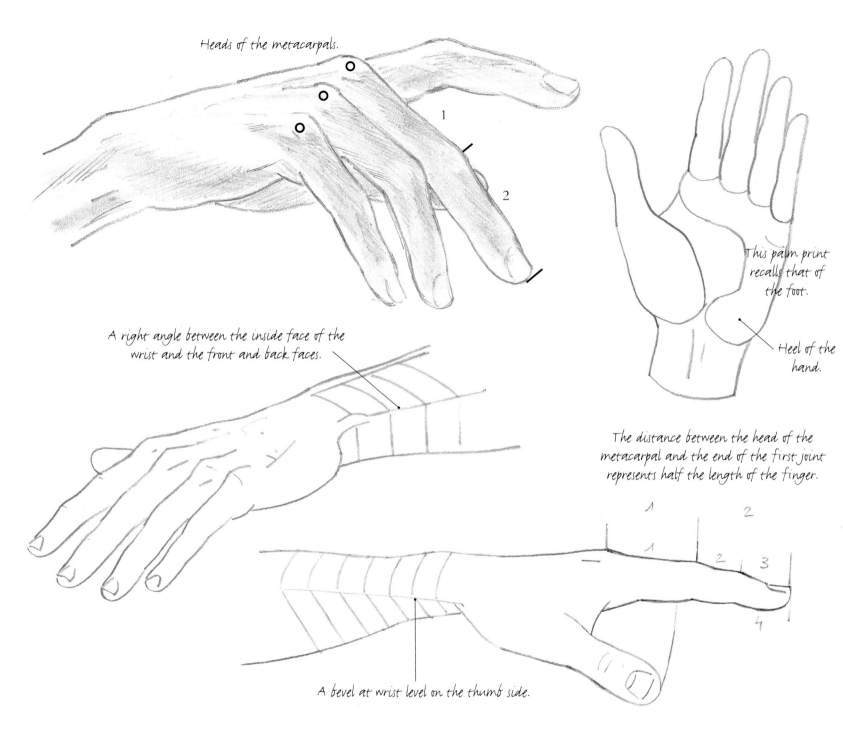

Heads of the metacarpals.

1

2

This palm print recalls that of the foot.

Heel of the hand.

A right angle between the inside face of the wrist and the front and back faces.

The distance between the head of the metacarpal and the end of the first joint represents half the length of the finger.

1   2

1   2   3

4

A bevel at wrist level on the thumb side.

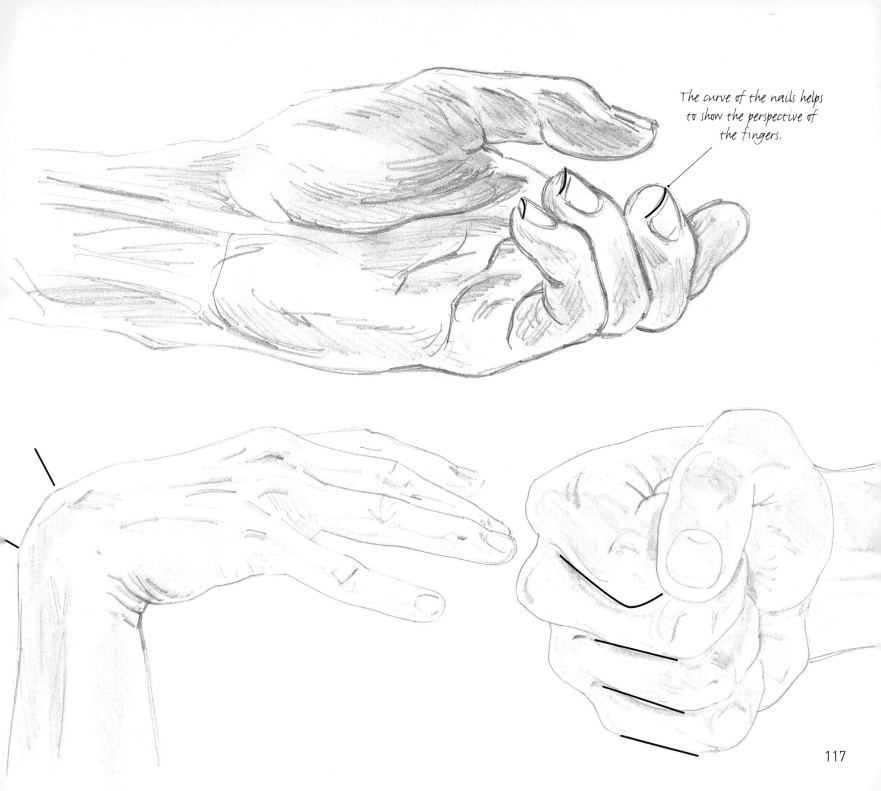

The curve of the nails helps to show the perspective of the fingers.

117

The ankle and the foot

On the outside and under the heel we find a thick rim of flesh compressed by the weight of the body. On the inside, an arch; at this point the foot is no longer in contact with the ground. The ankles, like the wrists, are subject to distortions linked to bending and stretching movements of the feet.

Concerning the foot

We can see an angle at the level of the big toe joint. This toe lies flat, while the others are often curved. At the level of the heel there are two masses, the highest corresponding to the heel bone (os calcis) and the other to the rim mentioned earlier.

The back of the foot is entirely composed of bones and tendons, with the exception of a fleshy muscle on the outside.

In this view from above we observe a slant in the ankle that reveals the forward position of the tibia.

Tibia.

Fibula.

small fleshy muscle.

Curved toes.

Big toe flat.

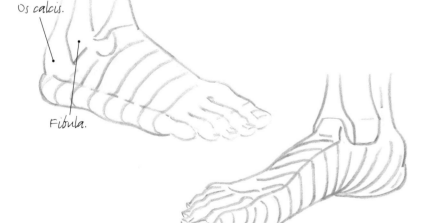

Os calcis.

Fibula.

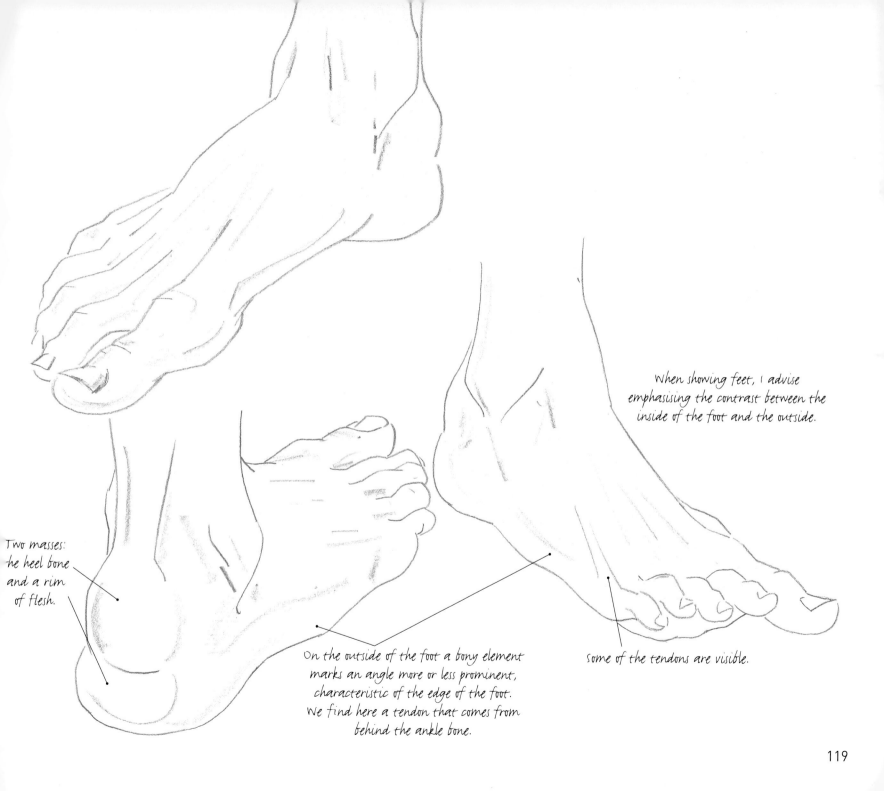

When showing feet, I advise emphasising the contrast between the inside of the foot and the outside.

Two masses: the heel bone and a rim of flesh.

On the outside of the foot a bony element marks an angle more or less prominent, characteristic of the edge of the foot. We find here a tendon that comes from behind the ankle bone.

some of the tendons are visible.

119

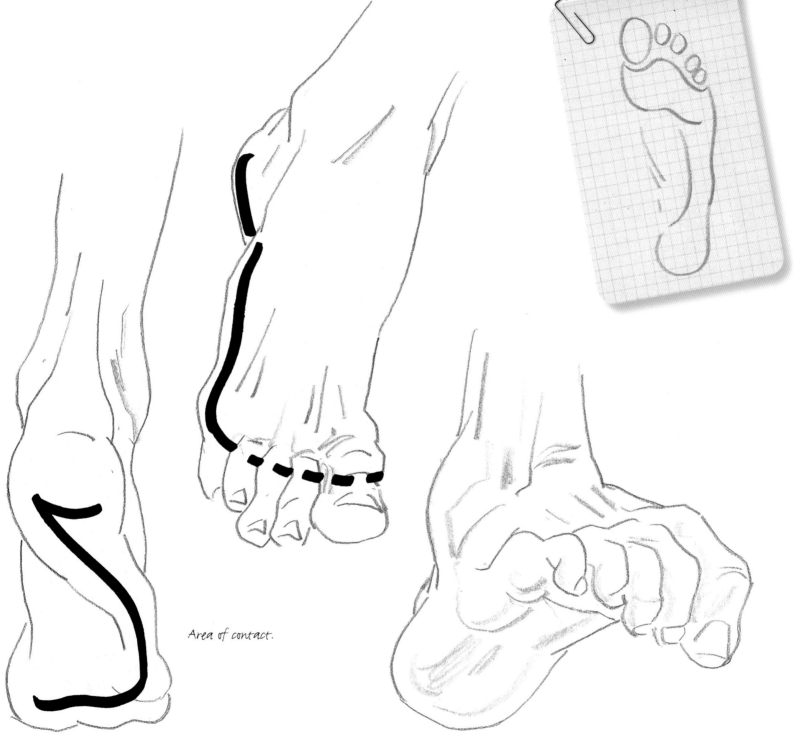

Area of contact.

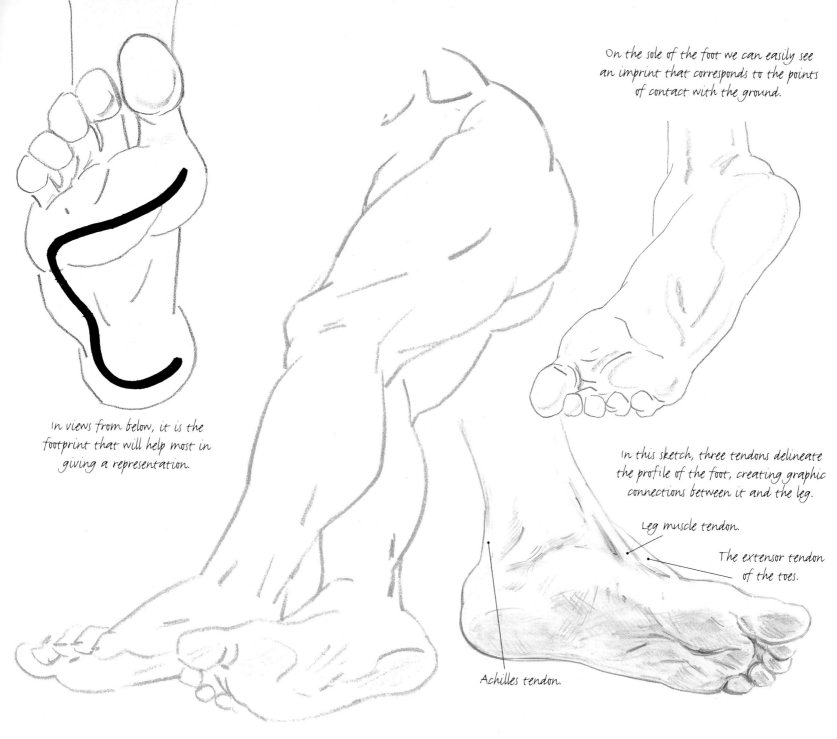

On the sole of the foot we can easily see an imprint that corresponds to the points of contact with the ground.

In views from below, it is the footprint that will help most in giving a representation.

In this sketch, three tendons delineate the profile of the foot, creating graphic connections between it and the leg.

Leg muscle tendon.

The extensor tendon of the toes.

Achilles tendon.

The body without skin

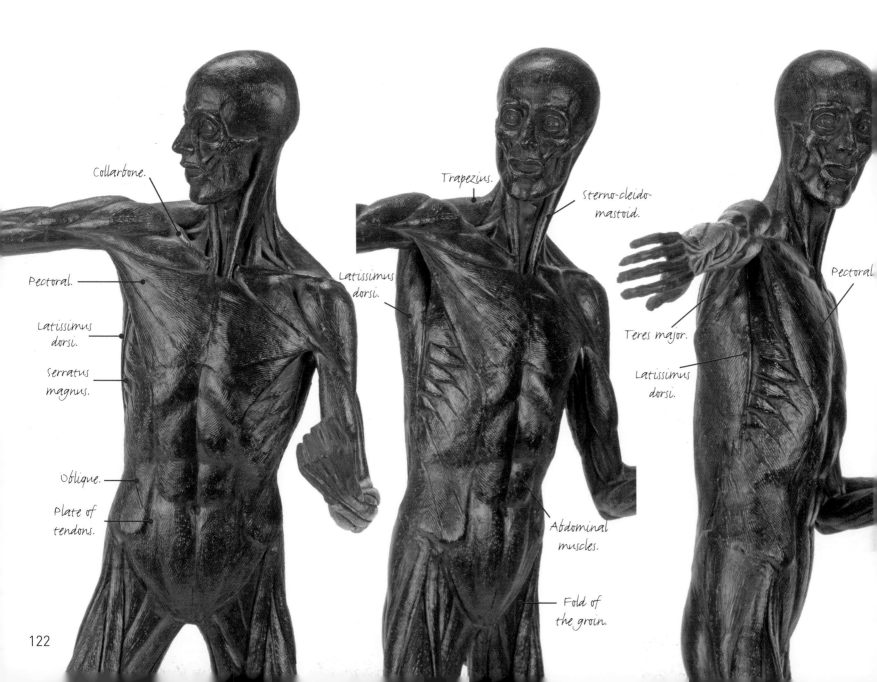

Collarbone.

Trapezius.

Sterno-cleido-
mastoid.

Pectoral.

Pectoral.

Latissimus
dorsi.

Latissimus
dorsi.

Teres major.

Serratus
magnus.

Latissimus
dorsi.

Oblique.

Abdominal
muscles.

Plate of
tendons.

Fold of
the groin.

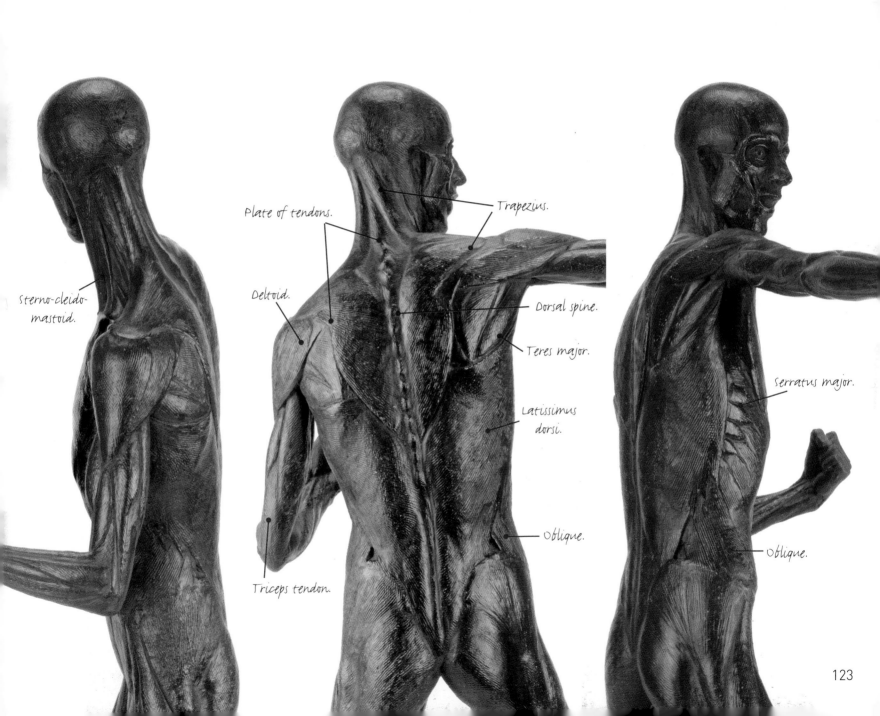

Sterno-cleido-
mastoid.

Plate of tendons.

Trapezius.

Deltoid.

Dorsal spine.

Teres major.

Latissimus
dorsi.

Serratus major.

Oblique.

Oblique.

Triceps tendon.

123

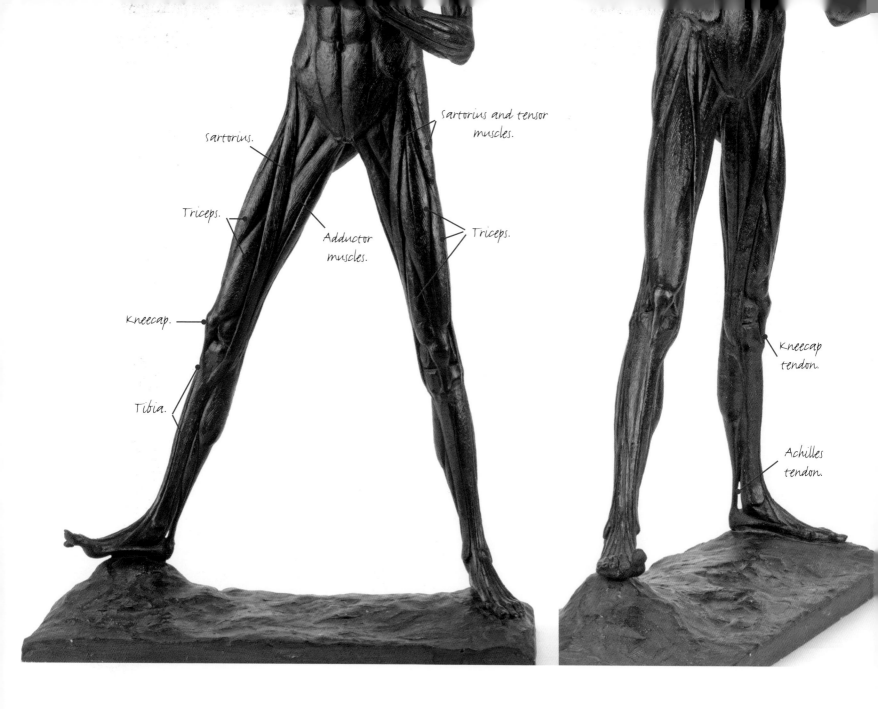

sartorius.

Sartorius and tensor
muscles.

Triceps.

Adductor
muscles.

Triceps.

Kneecap.

Kneecap
tendon.

Tibia.

Achilles
tendon.

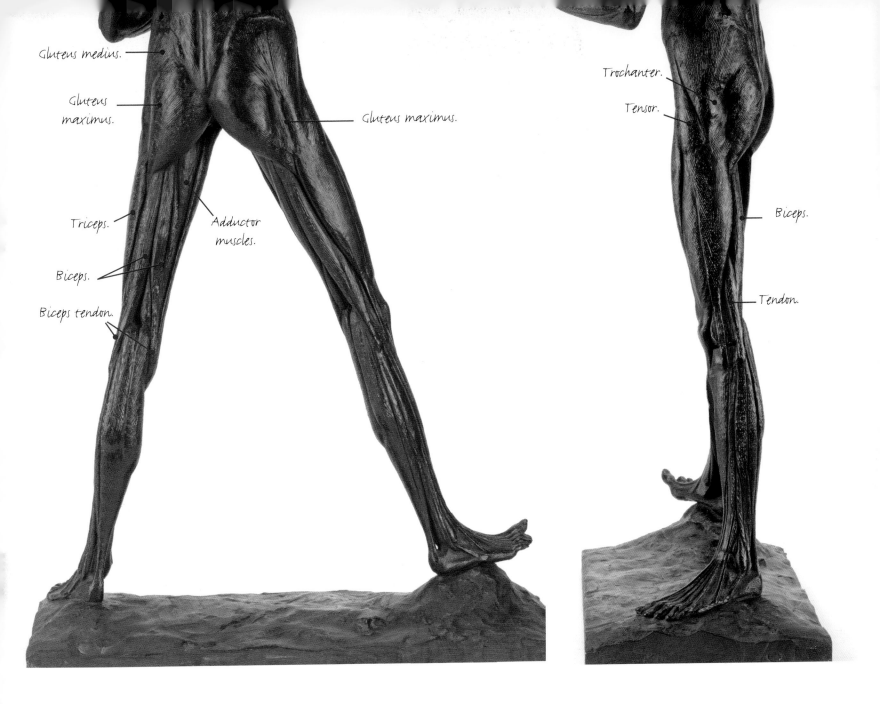

Gluteus medius.

Gluteus maximus.

Triceps.

Biceps.

Biceps tendon.

Adductor muscles.

Gluteus maximus.

Trochanter.

Tensor.

Biceps.

Tendon.

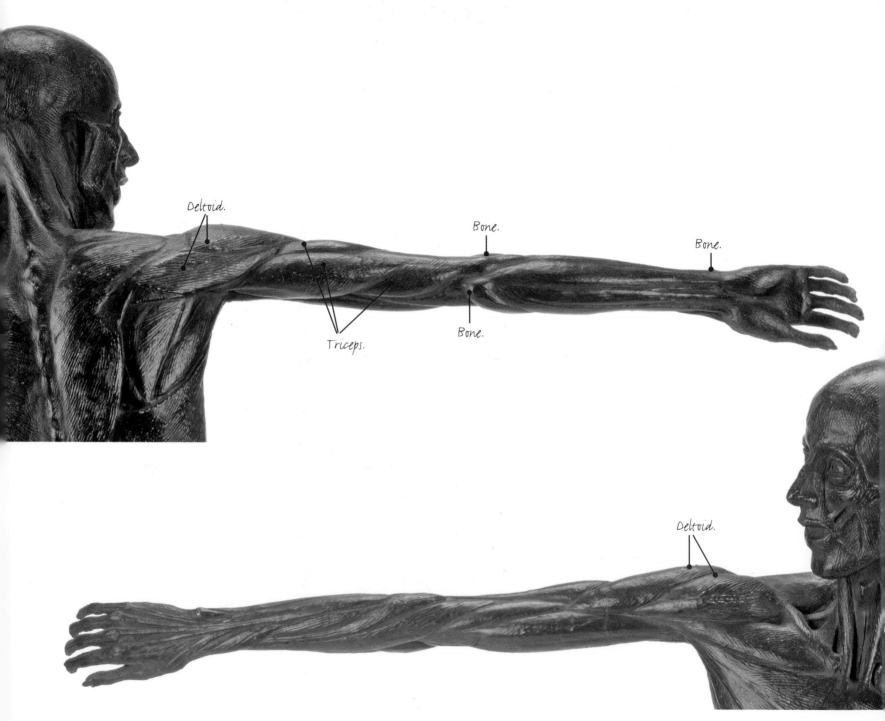

Deltoid.

Bone.

Bone.

Triceps.

Bone.

Deltoid.

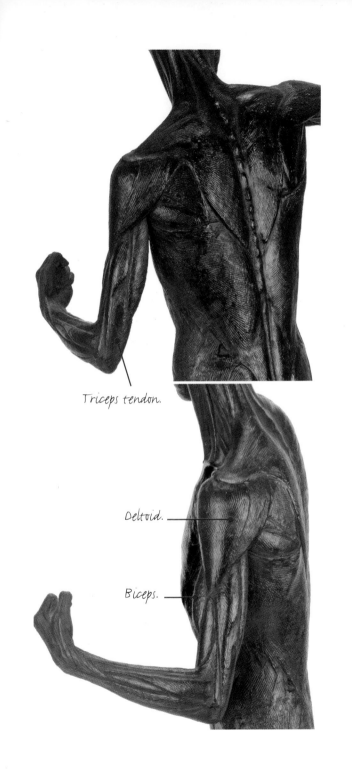

Triceps tendon.

Deltoid.

Biceps.

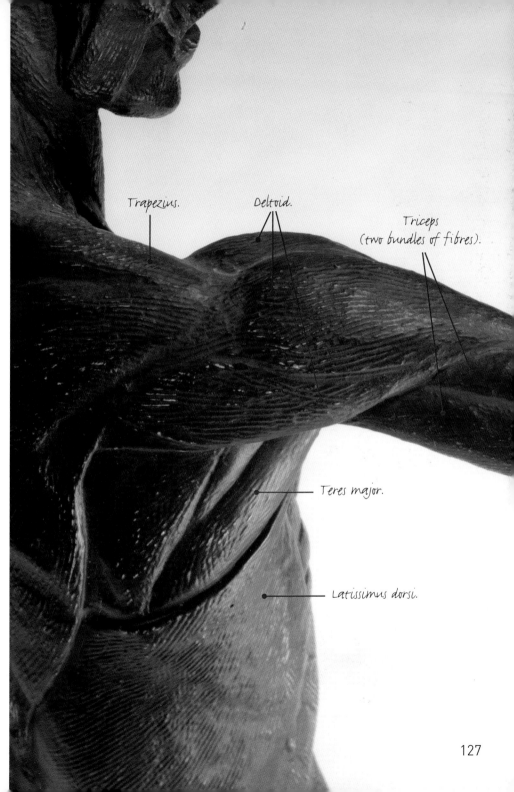

Trapezius.

Deltoid.

Triceps (two bundles of fibres).

Teres major.

Latissimus dorsi.

127